VOLUME 2

CHARACTER by GOD'S DESIGN

TRUST • HONESTY • OBEDIENCE

Group resources really work!

This Group resource incorporates our R.E.A.L. approach to ministry. It reinforces a growing friendship with Jesus, encourages long-term learning, and results in life transformation, because it's

Relational
Learner-to-learner interaction enhances learning and builds Christian friendships.

Experiential
What learners experience through discussion and action sticks with them up to 9 times longer than what they simply hear or read.

Applicable
The aim of Christian education is to equip learners to be both hearers and doers of God's Word.

Learner-based
Learners understand and retain more when the learning process takes into consideration how they learn best.

Character by God's Design, Volume 2
Copyright © 2016 Group Publishing, Inc.

Visit our website: **group.com**

CREDITS
Executive Editor: Christine Yount Jones
Assistant Editor: Ann Diaz
Senior Art Director: RoseAnne Sather
Print Production Artist: Amber Gomez Balanzar
Media Production Supervisor/Producer: Michael Freeman
Illustrators: Paige Billin-Frye, David Cabot, Wes Comer, Patrick Creyts, Pamela Johnson, Dana Regan, Ronnie Rooney, Drew Rose
Photographers: iStockphoto.com: Tammy Crosson, draconus, Jan Gottwald, Anna Kucherova, Thomas Perkins, toto8888

ISBN 978-1-4707-4217-1

Printed in the United States of America.

10 9 8 7 6 5 4 3 2 1   20 19 18 17 16

HOW TO USE
CHARACTER by G⦿D'S DESIGN

Character by God's Design is rooted in Scripture and engages kids to grow to be like Jesus. Use these lessons to equip kids with the character qualities they need to each become the person God created them to be. This second volume of exciting, hands-on Bible lessons features the three character qualities of trust, honesty, and obedience. Kids will explore each character quality in memorable activities that reinforce God's foundational plan for a fruitful Christian life.

With these lessons, you'll introduce kids of all ages to:

- **Trust**—Firm and confident belief

- **Honesty**—Telling the truth

- **Obedience**—Doing what I'm told to do

OVERVIEW CHART

This helpful chart gives you an overview of the lesson. Read "What Kids Do" first so you have the big picture of what will happen in your classroom with kids. Use the "What You'll Need" list to review and gather all the supplies you'll need for a great lesson.

DEVOTION FOR TEACHERS

Character by God's Design isn't just for children; it's for you, too! Romans 8:29 says that God chose you "to become like his Son." With this devotion, let God speak to your heart and challenge you to grow closer to Him.

BIBLE FOUNDATION FOR TEACHERS

Each lesson includes an in-depth look into the related Bible passage. Allow God's Spirit to work in your heart and mind as you study the Scripture in preparation for your lesson.

THE LESSON

Research shows that people remember most of what they do but only a fraction of what they hear—which means that kids learn best by doing. Kids will act out skits, make things, participate in creative prayers, play games, discover truths, and so much more. Each lesson has the following features, plus more.

GOD SIGHTINGS

Talk about ways you've each seen God at work, and praise Him!

BIBLE EXPERIENCE

Dive into the Scripture with kids. And learn by doing a unique activity to drive home "the point" (indicated by a thumbprint).

LIFE APPLICATION

Reinforce the message with an experience designed to help kids apply God's Word to their lives.

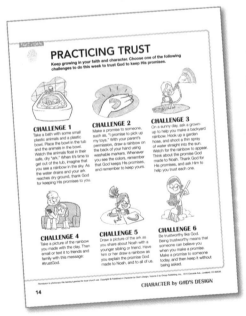

TAKE-HOME PAGE

Each week, kids will get six challenges on the Take-Home page. Encourage kids to choose at least one challenge to grow in character throughout the week. Let parents know that they can ask their children about the challenge and help when necessary.

TABLE OF CONTENTS

WE CAN TRUST GOD TO KEEP HIS PROMISES

TRUST IS...
firm and confident belief in someone.

Genesis 6:9–7:10;
8:13-17; 9:8-13:
God Sends a Rainbow

God flooded the earth but spared Noah's family by having him build the ark. Then God promised never to send another flood to cover the earth. That's just one of the many promises we can find in the Bible. When we learn about the promises of God, there's only one thing to do—trust Him. He'll always do what He says. Use this lesson to help children learn that we can trust God to keep His promises.

WHAT KIDS DO	WHAT YOU'LL NEED
God Sightings *(5 minutes)* Share ways they've seen God at work.	
Bible Experience *(10 minutes)* Interact with an account of Noah and the ark.	• Bible • spray bottle with water
Rainbow of Promises *(15 minutes)* Draw rainbows and learn about God's promises in the Bible.	• Bibles • copies of the handout *(found at the end of this lesson)* • crayons • pencils
Clay Rainbows *(5 minutes)* Make rainbows with clay and talk about God's promises.	• Bible • multi-colored clay
Who Can You Trust? *(15 minutes)* In pairs, do a trust walk around your classroom area.	• blindfolds for pairs • obstacles such as chairs and piles of books
Life Application *(10 minutes)* Talk about how flames are like promises.	• clean jar with lid • votive candle • long butane lighter • potholder

ILLUSTRATION BY PAIGE BILLIN-FRYE

Photocopy the Take-Home page at the end of this lesson for each child.

TRUST DEVOTION

How much more would we trust God in our everyday lives if we remembered that God always keeps His promises? The rainbow is just one of the many signs that God is faithful to His word, no matter what. At times we may want to second-guess God and try to take matters into our own hands, but instead we can rest in the knowledge that God will always keep His promises.

BIBLE FOUNDATION FOR TEACHERS

Genesis 6:9–7:10; 8:13-17; 9:8-13:
God Sends a Rainbow

SIN TAKES OVER

The sin begun by Adam and Eve multiplied even more in the generations that followed. The sin became so great, in fact, that the Bible describes the heart of humanity as "consistently and totally evil" (Genesis 6:5).

A DIFFICULT DECISION

God's statement that He'd wipe out the human race may seem as if it stemmed from anger or a desire for revenge, but instead it was a sorrowful acknowledgment that to make things better, most of the earth's population would have to die. The people God had created had turned completely against Him, so God decided to start over with the few who remained faithful.

ILLUSTRATION BY DANA REGAN

NOAH IS SAVED

Fortunately, one righteous man still loved God. God would save Noah, his wife, his three sons, and his sons' wives from the flood. God commanded Noah to build an ark that would house Noah's family and two of every kind of animal, so life could begin again after the floodwaters receded.

A BEAUTIFUL REMINDER

The Bible says the rain lasted 40 days and 40 nights, destroying every living thing on the earth. When the rain stopped and the water dried up, God established a covenant not only with Noah and his family, but also with every living thing that would ever walk the earth. God placed a beautiful rainbow in the sky as a promise to all humanity that He would never again destroy the earth with a flood. Even now, thousands of years later, we can see the sign of God's covenant after it rains and remember that God always keeps His promises.

GOD SIGHTINGS

As a group, share God Sightings—ways you've seen God at work. Then celebrate how God is at work in your lives through a prayer of thanksgiving.

BIBLE EXPERIENCE

Read aloud Genesis 6–9.

Tell children they can help you bring the Bible to life. Whenever they hear an animal mentioned, have them sound off with that animal's noise. For thunder, have them stomp their feet.

Say: **Many years ago, the earth was bad. Only a man named Noah was good. God told Noah that He would bring a flood of waters upon the earth to destroy everything. God told Noah to build an ark so that Noah, his family, and every living creature would survive.**

Noah obeyed. He built the ark and loaded the animals onto the ark. First came the dogs (*pause after each animal to allow noises*)**, then the cats, then the owls, then the lions, then the pigs, then the cows, then the chimpanzees, then the sheep, then the coyotes, then the horses, then the fruit flies, and finally the kangaroos. When all the animals were loaded, they made a noise that could be heard for miles.** (*Pause for animal noises.*) **Soon darkness covered the sky.** (*Turn off most of the lights.*)

Huge clouds began coming in from the north. They rolled slowly across the sky. Soon the skies were filled with clouds. Never before had anyone seen clouds like these.

Soon it began to lightning (*turn lights on and off rapidly*) **and thunder** (*stomp feet*)**. The animals became frightened and began to cry out.** (*All animals sound off.*)

Then came the rains. (*Mist water over their heads.*) **The rains continued and filled all the streams and rivers and**

THE LESSON

YOU'LL NEED:

✓ **Bible**
✓ **spray bottle with water**

FOR TEACHERS:
DOUBT CAN FEED FAITH

"Everyone at times can have doubts. But doubts don't change truth or upset God. Often when we can't see or feel something, we doubt if it's real. But just like air you can't see—God is there. Put another way, 'Faith is the assurance of things hoped for, the confidence in things not seen.' "
—John Trent in *Children's Ministry Magazine*

lakes and oceans. Finally the entire earth was covered with water.

After 40 days and 40 nights, the rains stopped. *(Stop water misting.)* **The clouds began moving back to where they came from. The sun began to shine** *(turn on lights)* **and the waters that covered the earth receded.**

When it was safe, Noah opened the door. Out came the chimpanzees *(pause after each animal),* **then the cats, and the dogs, then horses, cows, and the lions, then the owls, and the sheep, then the coyotes, the pigs, the fruit flies, and of course the kangaroos.**

God put a rainbow in the sky as a promise to never flood the earth again. God blessed Noah's family. Noah and his family and the animals all went forth to live a happy life as they replenished the earth.

Lead this discussion: **Why is God's promise to Noah important to us today? What can you learn about God from today's skit? Trust is firm and confident belief in someone— why can ● we trust God to keep His promises?**

RAINBOW OF PROMISES

Say: **After God flooded the earth, He promised Noah that He'd never do it again. Let's each make a rainbow to remember God's promises.** Distribute Bibles, handouts, and crayons. Lead kids through these steps, inviting volunteers to read aloud the verses.

Color a red arch to remember that red apples are good to eat. Read Philippians 4:19. Ask: **What is God's promise here?**

Color an orange arch to remember to be careful. Read Psalm 18:30. Ask: **What is God's promise here?**

Color a yellow arch like the sun. Read Hebrews 13:5. Ask: **What is God's promise here?**

Color a green arch to remember resting in the grass. Read Matthew 11:28. Ask: **What is God's promise here?**

✓ **Bibles**

✓ **copies of the handout (found at the end of this lesson)**

✓ **crayons**

✓ **pencils**

Color a blue and indigo arch to remember feeling sad. Read Psalm 55:22. Ask: **What is God's promise here?**

Color a purple or violet arch to think of someone you love. Read Romans 8:39. Ask: **What is God's promise here?**

Lead this discussion: **Which of God's promises means the most to you right now? Why do you trust that God will keep that promise in the future?**

Say: **The colors of the rainbow remind us that God keeps His promises to forgive us, help us, answer our prayers, love us no matter what, and never leave us. Just like Noah, we can trust God to keep His promises.**

CLAY RAINBOWS

Talk about: **God sent a rainbow for Noah to see as a reminder of His promise to never flood the earth again. The rainbow is a reminder of God's promise to us, too. We can trust God to keep His promises.**

Set out the colorful clay and let kids make rainbows to remind them of God's great promises.

As they're working, read aloud Psalm 33:4. Lead this discussion: **What does it mean to trust God? Which of God's promises is the easiest for you to trust? Which of God's promises is the most difficult for you to trust?**

Say: **This week, people may break or keep promises to you. But no matter what happens, you can trust God to keep His promises.**

WHO CAN YOU TRUST?

Have everyone get into pairs. Let the child wearing the most blue be the person in each pair to be blindfolded first. Once blindfolds are on, quickly make an obstacle course in the room with chairs and piles of books or other large objects.

Supervise as kids lead their blindfolded partners around your classroom area, making sure no one gets injured along the way.

YOU'LL NEED:

✓ **Bible**
✓ **multi-colored clay**

YOU'LL NEED:

✓ **blindfolds for pairs**
✓ **obstacles such as chairs and piles of books**

Then have them switch places so everyone gets a turn to be blindfolded. Rearrange some of the obstacles.

Afterward, lead this discussion: **What was it like to be blindfolded and to trust the other person? How does that compare to trusting God?**

LIFE APPLICATION

See the Teacher Prep box in advance of this activity.

Light the candle inside the jar. Say: **When someone makes a promise to us, we trust them to keep that promise. We're counting on them to follow through.**

Hold up the jar so kids can see the flames.

Say: **If the person making the promise lets us down, we can feel disappointed and it's hard to trust that person again.**

Place the lid over the top of the glass jar. Within a few seconds, the flame will run out of oxygen, dwindle, and go out.

Talk about: **This flame going out is like what happens when a promise is broken and we lose our trust in someone.**

Carefully remove the lid using a potholder. Then re-light the candle—this time leaving the lid off.

Say: **When God makes a promise, He never lets us down.** ◗ **We can trust God to keep His promises.**

Lead this discussion: **Tell about a time someone broke a promise to you. How was that like or unlike our candle experiment? How do we know that God won't break His promises?**

Talk about: **Think of our flame like trust between two people. When people make promises to each other, sometimes they keep those promises and the flame keeps burning, and sometimes they break the promises and the flame goes out. If someone breaks a promise to us, we**

have a hard time trusting that person to keep promises in the future. When God makes promises to us, He always keeps them. Our trust in God will never burn out! That's why  we can trust God to keep His promises.

PRAYER

Dear God, thank You for giving us so many wonderful promises. Help us learn to trust everything You do. In Jesus' name, amen.

TAKE-HOME PAGE

Give each child a Take-Home page to take home. Encourage kids to select one of the six challenges for the week ahead.

PRACTICING TRUST

Keep growing in your faith and character. Choose one of the following challenges to do this week to trust God to keep His promises.

CHALLENGE 1

Take a bath with some small plastic animals and a plastic bowl. Place the bowl in the tub and the animals in the bowl. Watch the animals float in their safe, dry "ark." When it's time to get out of the tub, imagine that you see a rainbow in the sky. As the water drains and your ark reaches dry ground, thank God for keeping His promises to you.

CHALLENGE 2

Make a promise to someone, such as, "I promise to pick up my toys." With your parent's permission, draw a rainbow on the back of your hand using washable markers. Whenever you see the colors, remember that God keeps His promises, and remember to keep yours.

CHALLENGE 3

On a sunny day, ask a grown-up to help you make a backyard rainbow. Hook up a garden hose, and shoot a thin spray of water straight into the sun. Watch for the rainbow to appear. Think about the promise God made to Noah. Thank God for His promises, and ask Him to help you trust each one.

CHALLENGE 4

Take a picture of the rainbow you made with the clay. Then email or text it to friends and family with this message: #trustGod.

CHALLENGE 5

Draw a picture of the ark as you share about Noah with a younger sibling or friend. Have him or her draw a rainbow as you explain the promise God made to Noah, and to all of us.

CHALLENGE 6

Be trustworthy like God. Being trustworthy means that someone can believe you when you make a promise. Make a promise to someone today, and then keep it without being asked.

RAINBOW OF PROMISES

Color a **RED** arch to remember that red apples are good to eat. Read Philippians 4:19. What is God's promise here?

_____

Color an **ORANGE** arch to remember to be careful. Read Psalm 18:30. What is God's promise here?

_____

Color a **YELLOW** arch like the sun. Read Hebrews 13:5. What is God's promise here?

_____

Color a **GREEN** arch to remember resting in the grass. Read Matthew 11:28. What is God's promise here?

_____

Color a **BLUE** and **INDIGO** arch to remember feeling sad. Read Psalm 55:22. What is God's promise here?

_____

Color a **PURPLE** or **VIOLET** arch to think of someone you love. Read Romans 8:39. What is God's promise here?

_____

LESSON 1 — WE CAN TRUST GOD TO KEEP HIS PROMISES

GOD IS PLEASED WHEN WE TRUST HIM

TRUST IS...
firm and confident belief in someone.

Genesis 22:1-18:
God Tests Abraham

Abraham trusted God, even when God asked him to sacrifice his son, Isaac. Abraham may have hoped God would provide another sacrifice and save Isaac, but was ready to sacrifice his son. And when God saved Isaac and sent a ram, Abraham was reminded that he could trust God. We, too, can trust God no matter what, because we know that God loves us. Use this lesson to help kids learn that God is pleased when we trust Him.

WHAT KIDS DO	WHAT YOU'LL NEED
God Sightings *(5 minutes)* Share ways they've seen God at work.	
Bible Experience *(10 minutes)* Learn what a flashlight can teach them about trust.	• Bible • flashlight • tape • paper clip
Trust Maze *(10 minutes)* Trust a partner to help them get through a maze.	• Bible • copies of the handout *(found at the end of this lesson)* • pencils
House of Trust *(10 minutes)* Try to draw a diagram, and relate that experience to trust.	• handouts from the previous activity • pencils
Trust It *(10 minutes)* Go on a trust hunt and discuss things in which you place your trust.	
Life Application *(10 minutes)* Watch a video about some kids who had to learn about trust.	• *Character by God's Design* DVD • DVD player

*Photocopy the Take-Home page at the end of this lesson for each child.

ILLUSTRATION BY DANA REGAN

TRUST DEVOTION

Trust doesn't show up instantaneously when we find ourselves in a tough spot; it must grow out of our daily interaction with God. So walk with Him today: Love Him, speak to Him in prayer, learn more about Him in Scripture, turn your thoughts to Him throughout the day. Let your trust grow.

BIBLE FOUNDATION FOR TEACHERS

Genesis 22:1-18: God Tests Abraham

HAND ME A Q-TIP!

Did I hear that right?! Abraham surely must have wondered if he was hallucinating when God told him to take his only son and "sacrifice him as a burnt offering." Genesis doesn't describe Abraham's emotions here. We don't know if Abraham tossed and turned all night, wrestling with his decision. We aren't told if he gazed at sleeping Isaac, agonizing over what to do. But before we read on, we must pause here and remember that Abraham wasn't a superhuman or automaton; he was a man with emotions and logic and natural human instincts. As a loving human father, this task God was asking him to perform went against every fiber of his being.

AN AGONIZING DECISION

Scripture provides us two clues into what Abraham may have wrestled with that night. Abraham may have held out hope that God ultimately wouldn't ask him to go through with the brutal act of killing his own son; he hints toward this idea when he tells Isaac, "God will provide a sheep for the burnt offering, my son." The writer of Hebrews gives us another insight into Abraham's mind-set: "Abraham reasoned that if Isaac died, God was able to bring him back to life again" (Hebrews 11:19).

ILLUSTRATION BY DANA REGAN

In both of these glimpses into Abraham's thoughts, we see trust. Though God was asking the most outrageous, unnatural, and indeed even horrifying thing, Abraham still found ways to trust God. He trusted that God could provide a sheep at the last minute; he trusted that if he did have to go through with the act, God could perform a miracle. Beyond all human reason clamoring for him to disobey, Abraham trusted God. And his trust was not misplaced; God did come through, providing a ram to be sacrificed. Abraham passed this gut-wrenching test of faith.

GOT TRUST?

We naturally trust those we know and love. Abraham knew God and loved Him. He'd already walked through some difficult situations with God; he'd already been amazed by God's promises and miracles many times. It was out of this relationship—this sense of knowing God's character—that Abraham was able to base his trust. Similarly, our trust for God flows out of our relationship with Him. As we grow to know and love God more deeply and intimately and as we walk with Him daily through the ups and downs of life, trust grows. Though we most likely won't face a choice as awful as Abraham's, there will be times God asks us to step out in faith. Like Abraham, we can choose to trust in God and His character.

THE LESSON

GOD SIGHTINGS

As a group, share God Sightings—ways you've seen God at work. Then celebrate how God is at work in your lives through a prayer of thanksgiving.

BIBLE EXPERIENCE

See the Teacher Prep box on the next page in advance of this activity.

Ask kids to talk about hard things they've had to do. Then say: **A man named Abraham trusted God with a hard thing and that pleased God.** ◉ **God is pleased when we trust Him, too.**

Show the flashlight and batteries. Say: **I took apart a flashlight. As you see, these parts don't do anything if they're not connected.**

Let's say these two pieces are God and Abraham. In Genesis 22:1-18, God asked Abraham to obey Him. Read verses 1-2. **Abraham trusted God to know what was best.** Read verse 3. **Trust** (indicate the paper clip) **connected Abraham to God.**

YOU'LL NEED:

✓ **Bible**
✓ **flashlight**
✓ **tape**
✓ **paper clip**

Take off the front end of the flashlight. Take the batteries out of the flashlight, and straighten the paper clip. Tape the batteries together, side by side. You will hold the positive end of one of the batteries to the metal dot or wire at the base of the light bulb while a child holds the paper clip to both the negative end of the battery and the metal disk in the bulb piece. Help the child bend the paper clip so that the ends can touch easily and simultaneously.

YOU'LL NEED:

✓ **Bible**

✓ **copies of the handout** (found at the end of this lesson)

✓ **pencils**

Read verses 4-6. **In that time, people sacrificed animals to show their devotion to God. This day, God told Abraham to sacrifice his beloved son, Isaac.** Connect the batteries and the front end of the flashlight. Let a child help.

The light shows us the current of trust flowing between these two friends. Tell about a friend you trust. Allow time; then disconnect the batteries and read verses 7-10.

Abraham trusted God so much that he did exactly what God said. Read verses 11-13. **And God honored Abraham's trust by providing an animal—instead of Isaac—for the sacrifice.**

Abraham's trust for God was strong, like a bright light, so God blessed Abraham. Abraham became the father of all nations!

Lead this discussion: **Why do you think Abraham trusted God? Tell about a time you trusted God. How has trusting God brought good things or light into your life?**

Talk about: **Trusting God brings light into our lives. If you spend time knowing and loving God like Abraham did, there's trust.** ● **God is pleased when we trust Him.**

TRUST MAZE

Say: **It must've been really hard for Abraham to let go of something he loved—his son—and trust God. But Abraham learned he could trust God. God will always love us, so we don't need to be afraid to trust Him.** ● **God is pleased when we trust Him.**

Read Hebrews 11:17-19. Ask: **What do these verses tell you about how Abraham trusted God?**

Say: **Let's do an activity to remind us that God wants us to trust Him in everything we do.**

Have kids get into pairs, and give everyone a handout and a pencil. Read the directions on the top half of the handout together. Have kids folds their papers so they don't accidentally write on the bottom half.

Allow a couple minutes for the first set of kids to get through the handout maze without looking. Then call time and have partners switch roles.

Afterward, lead this discussion: **How much did you trust that your partner could help you get through the maze? How does knowing and loving someone help us trust that person? How does knowing and loving God help us trust Him?**

HOUSE OF TRUST

Say: **Abraham showed that he trusted God, even though it must have been hard. And when God saved Isaac and sent a ram to be sacrificed, Abraham was reminded that he could trust God.**

Talk about: **Think about a time it was hard for you to trust God.** Give some examples, such as when families are moving or a pet dies. Invite volunteers to share. Then continue.

Abraham faced a tough challenge when God told him to sacrifice Isaac. What tough challenges are you facing right now?

Say: **Let's see if you can tackle this challenge! On the bottom half of your paper, draw the house diagram in the blank space without lifting your pencil or tracing over a line you've already drawn.**

After a minute, ask: **How'd you do? Keep trying to see if you can get it. This is possible!** After another minute, show kids the solution from the margin of this page.

Lead this discussion: **What made it so hard to solve this puzzle? What would be something that would be hard for you to do if God asked you to? How can you trust God as much as Abraham did?**

Say: **Abraham trusted God in a really big way, and we can trust God, too. This week remember that ● God is pleased when we trust Him.**

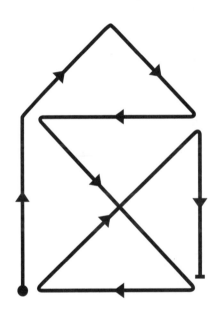

TRUST IT!

Go on a trust hunt together. Look around your church (go outside, too, if the weather's nice) and list things you see that you have to trust, such as a chair to be able to hold your weight, a vending machine to correctly give you the chosen snack, or a traffic light to work properly.

Talk about the things you've found that require your trust. Discuss how you may have been let down by things or people you've trusted.

Explain that even though sometimes humans and machines fail us, God never does. We can always trust God.

YOU'LL NEED:

✓ *Character by God's Design* **DVD**

✓ **DVD player**

LIFE APPLICATION

Say: **Sometimes trusting means putting your entire life on the line. Check out how these kids learned about trust.**

 Play "100-Foot Fall" (track 1) on the *Character by God's Design* DVD.

Afterward, lead this discussion: **What surprised you about this family and how they reacted to the accident? Tell about a time you faced a challenge to trust God. Why do you know you can trust God, even in really hard times?**

Talk about: **Trusting others can be hard—especially when we've been let down in the past. The family in our video had a really difficult time when the dad had an accident, but they trusted God to get them through it—and they still trust Him day by day. ● God is pleased when we trust Him, too. God loves us and will take care of us.**

PRAYER
Thank You, God, for always being faithful to us. Thank You that we can trust You. Please help us remember that You never leave us, and help us trust You more. In Jesus' name, amen.

TAKE-HOME PAGE

Give each child a Take-Home page to take home. Encourage kids to select one of the six challenges for the week ahead.

PRACTICING TRUST

Keep growing in your faith and character. Choose one of the following challenges to do this week to show you trust God.

CHALLENGE 1

When you go up any stairs this week, remember that Abraham trusted God as he walked up the mountain to sacrifice his son. When you reach the top, remember how God rewarded Abraham's trust. Then say, "God is pleased when I trust in Him."

CHALLENGE 2

Ask a parent to tie a piece of yarn around your wrist as a bracelet. Use the yarn as a reminder to talk to God when you're afraid or unsure.

CHALLENGE 3

Gather photos or draw pictures of the people you're closest to, such as family members or best friends. Name reasons you trust those people. Compare those reasons to the reasons you can trust God. Then put the pictures or drawings in your room to remind you to trust God the way you trust those people.

CHALLENGE 4

Think about a friend who is having a hard time right now. Connect with that friend and tell him or her about Abraham. Then offer to pray for your friend, and encourage your friend to trust God the way Abraham did.

CHALLENGE 5

Make a list of some things you have. Write how you get each of these things, tracing back as far as you can go until you get to God. (For example, for "water," you would write water—faucet—underground city pipes—reservoir—rain water—God.) Note how many things you can trust God to provide for you.

CHALLENGE 6

Write one thing you're worried about and you want to trust God to take care of for you. Fold the paper and then pray to God about that thing, and put it away somewhere. Each time you feel yourself worry, remember that the worry is folded up and put away.

MAZE AND LINE PUZZLE

INSTRUCTIONS: Set your pencil at the starting point of the maze. Close your eyes as you try to get to center of the maze. Your partner will use words to guide you. Then switch roles and guide your partner through the maze.

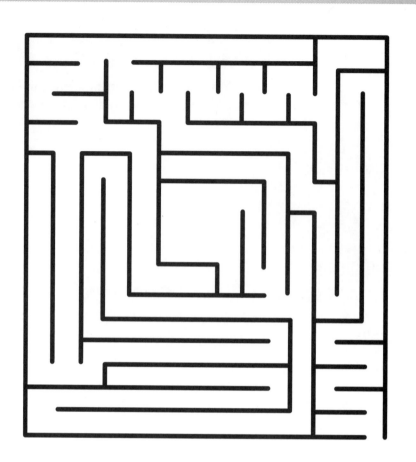

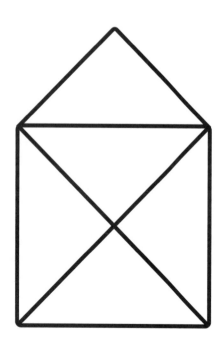

DRAW THE HOUSE HERE

WE CAN LOOK TO GOD FOR HELP

TRUST IS...
firm and confident belief in someone.

Exodus 15:22-26:
The Israelites Drink
Bitter Water

We can go to God for help just as the Israelites went to God for help when they were thirsty in the desert and had only bitter water to drink. God led them to that water and when Moses asked for help, God told Moses how to sweeten the water. Use this lesson to help children learn that no matter how big or how small the problem, we can always go to God for help.

WHAT KIDS DO	WHAT YOU'LL NEED
God Sightings *(5 minutes)* Share ways they've seen God at work.	
Bible Experience *(10 minutes)* Watch a video about God helping Moses and the Israelites.	• Bible • *Character by God's Design* DVD • DVD player
Bead Protection *(10 minutes)* Think of someone they trust, and see if tape will keep beads dry.	• Bible • alphabet beads *(available at craft stores)* • masking tape • cups of water
Stop, Drop, and Pray *(10 minutes)* Run in place as they learn about prayer as an aspect of trust.	
Prayer Wall *(10 minutes)* Create a wall full of prayers, and then pray together for each of them.	• pads of sticky notes • markers
Life Application *(15 minutes)* Lead partners on a course of trust.	• masking tape • string

ILLUSTRATION BY DREW ROSE

*Photocopy the Take-Home page at the end of this lesson for each child.

TRUST DEVOTION

Just as God was faithful in taking care of the Israelites, He'll be faithful in taking care of us. Although God doesn't promise there won't be hard times, He does promise to get us through them and provide us with what we need. Jesus told his disciples, "I tell you not to worry about everyday life" (Matthew 6:25). Remember to look to God for help, no matter how dire the situation may seem.

BIBLE FOUNDATION FOR TEACHERS

Exodus 15:22-26: The Israelites Drink Bitter Water

A DIRE NEED

Three days after God led the Israelites through the Red Sea on dry land, the people grew anxious about their lack of water supply. They were traveling hundreds of miles through a vast wilderness, and it was necessary for them to constantly replenish their water sources.

BITTER WATER

The Israelites finally found a water supply, only to discover that it was too bitter to drink. Instead of trusting in the mighty God who had delivered them from Egypt and brought them through the Red Sea, the people complained to Moses about their situation.

GOD PROVIDES

Moses acted as the messenger between God and the people of Israel, so he pleaded with God to provide water for them to drink. The Lord gave Moses the answer: Throw a piece of wood in the water. And the water was immediately suitable for drinking.

A POWERFUL REMINDER

The passage continues with God's decree to the Israelites, in which God told them that He wanted their continual obedience and respect. In return, God promised He would take care of them and keep them free from all the diseases that had been inflicted on the Egyptians as part of the plagues. It seems that even though God had shown the Israelites His power many times before, they still needed a reminder that if they followed God and trusted Him, He would care for their needs.

GOD SIGHTINGS

As a group, share God Sightings—ways you've seen God at work. Then celebrate how God is at work in your lives through a prayer of thanksgiving.

BIBLE EXPERIENCE

Read aloud Exodus 15:22-26.

Talk about: **Have you ever faced a really serious situation and didn't know who to turn to? It can be scary when you don't know who to go to for help. The Bible tells us that while Moses was leading the Israelites in the desert, they had a big problem. But God helped Moses and the Israelites. Just like Moses, we can look to God for help, no matter what our problem is.**

Play "Sweet-a-Stick" (track 2) on the *Character by God's Design* DVD.

Afterward, lead this discussion: **What surprised you about how God helped Moses? Tell about a time someone helped you do something. How can you look to God for help the way you looked to that person for help?**

Say: **There's no such thing as a Sweet-a-Stick. Only God could do the miracle He did to make bitter water taste good. When the Israelites complained to Moses, he looked to God for help. When we have times where it would be easy to give up, we can look to God for help, too.**

BEAD PROTECTION

Say: **When God's people, the Israelites, were in the desert, they became very thirsty. Moses looked to God for help, and God showed him what to do to help the Israelites.**

Gather everyone around the beads. Say: **Think of one or two people you trust. Remember that trust is firm and confident belief in someone. Find the beads to spell the name of someone you trust.**

THE LESSON

YOU'LL NEED:

✓ **Bible**
✓ ***Character by God's Design* DVD**
✓ **DVD player**

YOU'LL NEED:

✓ **Bible**
✓ **alphabet beads *(available at craft stores)***
✓ **masking tape**
✓ **cups of water**

Help kids find beads. Then say: **We can trust friends, family, and other things, but we can trust God more than anyone or anything.**

Read Psalm 33:4. Talk about: **What does this verse say about trusting God?**

Have kids use masking tape to wrap up their alphabet beads so they'll stay dry, and give everyone a cup of water for immersing the beads. Then say: **Ready? Drop the tape-protected beads in the water and count to 30.**

Have kids take the alphabet beads out of the water, take off the tape, and feel how dry they are.

Lead this discussion: **How much did you trust that the tape would keep the beads dry? Think about a time you were afraid and didn't know what was going to happen. How did you or could you have trusted God in that situation? Why do you think God wants us to look to Him for help?**

Say: **Moses showed the Israelites how to look to God for help. When we're afraid or discouraged, or when we don't know what to do, ● we can look to God for help. We can trust God and everything He does.**

STOP, DROP AND PRAY

Say: **When Moses looked to God for help in the desert, God showed him what to do to help the Israelites. God turned the bitter water into sweet water so the Israelites would have something to drink.**

One way to look to God for help is in prayer. When can you pray to God? Let's get energized and find out!

Have kids stand in a circle. Give these directions: **Run in place as I read this story about a make-believe day in your life. When I say, "Stop, drop, and pray," I want you to say it with me, and when you do, stop running, drop to your knees, and put your hands together in prayer. Then hop back on your feet and run again! Ready? Let's go!**

Read this story slowly:

You get up in the morning and have breakfast. Before you eat, you stop, drop, and pray. At school, you have a quiz. Stop, drop, and pray. Later, your dad calls you in for a chat. Stop, drop, and pray. After school, you want to play with your best friend, but he's very sick. Stop, drop, and pray. Then, you and your sister get into a fight over the TV. Stop, drop, and pray. You head to bed, worried about tomorrow. Stop, drop, and pray.

Lead this discussion: **What things make you stop, drop, and pray right away? Think about a time you were in trouble and needed help... How did God help you with that problem?**

Say: **Just like the Israelites, ● we can look to God for help, and He'll give it to us. When we need help, we can stop, drop, and pray as our first response, and God will always be there to help us.**

PRAYER WALL

YOU'LL NEED:

✓ **pads of sticky notes**
✓ **markers**

Place pads of sticky notes and markers next to a wall. Ask kids to write prayer requests on the sticky notes. Allow several minutes for them to create a "prayer wall" by sticking the notes to the wall.

Look to God for help as you pray together for the things written on the wall.

PRAY FOR
AUNT
SUE
IN THE HOSPITAL

LIFE APPLICATION

YOU'LL NEED:

✓ **masking tape**
✓ **string**

See the Teacher Prep box on the next page in advance of this activity.

Form pairs. Say: **We have a challenge before us! Like Moses and the people in the desert, sometimes we have to travel from point A to point B, and the way's not always easy. You're going to travel across the wilderness in pairs. One of you will be the Traveler and the other will be the Helper; then you'll switch. Here's the catch: The Traveler will have to keep his or her eyes closed on the journey.**

Have pairs line up at one end of the path. Say: **We're going to travel across and back while the Traveler keeps his or her**

eyes closed. On the way across, the Helper should walk on the side of the Traveler and talk the Traveler through the course, saying things such as "right," "left," "keep coming," or "stop." On the way back, the Traveler and Helper will switch roles. This time, the Helper can guide the Traveler with a short string. Hand out strings to pairs, and allow time for everyone to navigate the paths.

Lead this discussion: **What did you do when you needed help on the path? Explain whether you trusted your Helper more or less than you trust God. What things can you trust God to help you with in your life?**

Talk about: **It may have been hard to trust your helper to help you follow such a zigzagging path. Moses and the Israelites had trouble trusting God after walking through the desert for three days without finding water. But they looked to God and He brought them to water and made the water drinkable.** ● **We can look to God for help when we're lost or confused, too.**

PRAYER
Dear God, thank You for being strong and powerful and for helping us. Please remind us to look to You this week whenever we need help. In Jesus' name, amen.

TAKE-HOME PAGE

Give each child a Take-Home page to take home. Encourage kids to select one of the six challenges for the week ahead.

PRACTICING TRUST

Keep growing in your faith and character. Choose one of the following challenges to do this week to look to God for help.

CHALLENGE 1

Get a glass of water. As you drink it, silently pray that God would help you look to Him for help with your big and little needs this week. Then thank God for something you know He's already helped you with.

CHALLENGE 2

Write "LOOK" on a card. Make eyes in the two O's, and add a smile below the eyes. Put the card in a place where you'll see it often and remember to look to God for help this week.

CHALLENGE 3

Use popsicle sticks and glue to make an arrow. Set it up in your bathroom, pointing up. When you see it, say aloud, "I can look to God for help." Then apply what you say to what's currently going on in your life.

CHALLENGE 4

Read Matthew 7:7-8. Remember that we can look to God for help, and write on a piece of paper what the verses in Matthew 7 tell us to do. Next, write three things you'd like God to help you with. Throughout the day, focus on the things you listed and do what the verse says.

CHALLENGE 5

Go outdoors and look at all of God's creations. Look at the trees, flowers, birds, animals, insects,clouds, and sky. Think about how well God takes care of them—if He takes care of even the birds and flowers, how much more will He take care of you? Pray to God and tell Him you'll trust Him and always look to Him for help.

CHALLENGE 6

Use pipe cleaners to make two pairs of glasses. Give one to a friend, and wear the glasses as you tell your friend what you learned about looking to God for help. Ask your friend what he or she wants to look to God for help with, and pray with your friend. Tell your friend to keep the glasses—when either of you needs help, you can put them on and pray to God.

WE TRUST GOD'S TIMING

TRUST IS...
firm and confident belief in someone.

1 Samuel 16:13-23: David Plays His Harp for Saul

King Saul was tormented by depression and fear. His servants brought David to play the harp for him because David was a man of God and a skilled musician. The music soothed Saul, so he kept David in his service. Though David knew God had chosen him to be king, he patiently waited for the right time and faithfully served Saul. Use this lesson to teach kids that we can trust God's timing.

WHAT KIDS DO	WHAT YOU'LL NEED
God Sightings *(5 minutes)* Share ways they've seen God at work.	
Bible Experience *(15 minutes)* Watch a video about David and Saul.	• Bible • *Character by God's Design* DVD • DVD player
Elementary *(20 minutes)* Learn about waiting on God by waiting on a snack.	• instant pudding mix • milk • graham crackers • large spoon and bowl • cups and plastic spoons
Slaphands *(10 minutes)* Play a hand-slapping game in pairs and talk about timing.	
Life Application *(10 minutes)* Use coins to learn about patience.	• coin for each child

ILLUSTRATION BY PAMELA JOHNSON

*Photocopy the Take-Home page at the end of this lesson for each child.

33

TRUST DEVOTION

Have you ever been in God's waiting room? It's tough to pray and wait for days, weeks, months...even years for answers. It's hard to rely on God as you wait for a career change or a clean bill of health or a spouse or a new child. The way you choose to wait reveals the trust you have in God. This week, wait in an attitude of surrender, exhibiting your belief that God is in control and His timing is best.

BIBLE FOUNDATION FOR TEACHERS

1 Samuel 16:13-23: David Plays His Harp for Saul

CHOSEN

After Saul's display of halfhearted devotion and partial obedience, God told Samuel, "I am sorry that I ever made Saul king" (1 Samuel 15:11). Samuel "cried out to the Lord" all night, realizing that God had rejected Saul. Soon afterward, God put into motion His plan to select the new king; He sent Samuel to the home of Jesse in Bethlehem. Samuel looked at all of Jesse's sons—none of the tall, handsome, mature sons fit the bill. Jesse then sent for his youngest boy, David, and God told Samuel, "This is the one; anoint him" (1 Samuel 16:12). Even though Saul was reigning as king over Israel, Samuel anointed David as the chosen ruler for God's people.

HONORED

Immediately after the account of David's anointing, we're drawn back into the palace, where Saul was now an absolute mess. Scripture describes the king as being tormented by a "spirit"— he suffered from bouts of intense depression and fear. Saul's servants told the tortured king about a talented musician from Bethlehem: a boy, Jesse's son David. Saul sent for David, asking him to serve in the royal court by playing soothing music during the king's darkest episodes. David served Saul so well that Scripture says, "Saul loved David very much."

A MATTER OF TIMING

Apparently, Saul was completely unaware that Samuel had anointed David as king; if he'd known, he'd likely have seen the act as high treason. But David *did* know he was the future king, chosen by God. What did he do with that knowledge? He tucked

ILLUSTRATION BY PAIGE BILLIN-FRYE

it away, in complete trust and reliance on God, waiting for God's perfect timing. David trusted in God's authority—and he expressed that trust by honoring the current king, Saul.

David ended up having to wait a long time and endure a lot of hardship—including Saul's later campaign to hunt him down and kill him—until the moment finally arrived when God put him on the throne. Through all that waiting, David continued to show honor to Saul as he relied on and trusted in God's timing.

THE LESSON

GOD SIGHTINGS

As a group, share God Sightings—ways you've seen God at work. Then celebrate how God is at work in your lives through a prayer of thanksgiving.

BIBLE EXPERIENCE

Read aloud 1 Samuel 16:13-23.

Talk about: **God is never late—although sometimes we might feel He waits until the last possible second to answer our prayers! God has a plan for each of us and our lives, so we trust God's timing.**

Tell children about a time that you needed to trust God's timing.

Talk about: **David was a great man—but he was also a great kid. The things he did as a kid were just as impressive as those he did when he was king. In fact, one of the most impressive things he did wasn't defeating a giant—it was helping King Saul relax. Take a look.**

 Play "Harp Hero" (track 3) on the *Character by God's Design* DVD.

Afterward, lead this discussion: **Why do you think David didn't just tell King Saul that he was going to be the new king? God gave David the gift of music—what gifts has He given you? In what ways can you honor people with your gifts?**

Talk about: **Even though David knew he was going to be king, he still helped King Saul relax by playing the harp. David didn't try to take the crown away from King Saul,** because he knew that God had a plan. In the same way,  we trust God's timing.

SNACK TIME

Say: **Though David knew God had chosen him to be king, he patiently waited for the right time and faithfully served Saul. David trusted God's timing, and we can do the same.**

Have kids share their response to this question with a partner: **What's something you're looking forward to, and what are you doing while you wait?** Allow a couple minutes for this discussion; remind kids partway through to make sure they've each had a chance to share.

Then say: **Time to make a snack. Or, maybe I should say, "This snack will take time." Prepare to wait!**

Gather kids around the pudding supplies. Pour the pudding mix and milk in a bowl. Have kids take turns helping you stir. Ask: **Is it ready yet?** Continue stirring until the mixture is blended and smooth, and put into cups. Use graham crackers for dipping.

Lead this discussion: **Why was it a good idea to wait until the snack was ready before eating it? What might have happened if David had tried to be king while Saul was still king? Why do you think it is or isn't a good idea to trust God's timing?**

Say: **Sometimes we have to wait for things, as David did, even though waiting is hard. But timing is important. Like our pudding snack, some things just won't work out right unless we wait for the right time. God always knows the perfect time. That's why**  **we trust God's timing.**

SLAPHANDS

Have kids get into pairs to play this game of Slaphands. Ask for a volunteer to help you demonstrate.

Hold out your hands, palms up. Have your volunteer hold out his or her hands, palms down, over yours so your palms are close together.

- ✓ **instant pudding mix**
- ✓ **milk**
- ✓ **graham crackers**
- ✓ **large spoon and bowl**
- ✓ **cups and plastic spoons**

ALLERGY ALERT

Food allergies can be dangerous and even life-threatening. Consult with parents and be aware of any allergies the kids in your group might have.

Explain these directions: **Flip your hands over quickly and try to slap the backs of the other person's hands with your palms. The other person will try to pull his or her hands away before you can do it. If you successfully slap the person's hands or if the other person pulls away before you move, you win. If the other person successfully pulls his or her hands away after you move at all, he or she wins.**

Give everyone a chance to play Slaphands with one another.

Discuss how, when trying to pull your hands away, you had to pull them away at just the right time. Then lead this discussion: **What's something you wish God would do more quickly in your life? Why might He be waiting? Tell about a time that God's timing was faster than you were expecting. What's it like to do what God asks even if you aren't ready?**

Say: **Even when it's hard, it's important that ● we trust God's timing.**

LIFE APPLICATION

Have kids stand, and give each child a coin.

Say: **You can always tell who's king or queen by who's wearing the crown. For those future kings and queens among us, it's time to practice putting on your crowns! I'll toss my coin up and let it land on my head. You do the same with your own "crown"—your coin.**

Have children toss their coins up in the air and try to "catch" them on top of their heads. Ask kids to predict how many tries it will take to do this. Tell kids to make as many attempts as they'd like in 60 seconds.

After 60 seconds, say: **Why don't you try a different spot in the room, in case it works better there?** Allow another 30 seconds of trying, and then say: **Why don't you try trading your crown with someone else, in case yours isn't the right size?** Allow another 30 seconds. Then applaud everyone, and collect the coins.

Lead this discussion: **Describe your crown-tossing style. Tell about a time you thought something would be easy to do but it turned out to be hard. Talk about something that's hard for you now, but will be easier when you get older.**

Talk about: **You learn as you get older. There will be things you can do a year from now that you can't do today. But sometimes we're impatient. We don't want to wait a year. We want things now instead of letting God be in charge and trusting God's timing. It's better, though, if ● we trust God's timing.**

PRAYER
Dear God, help us be patient and trust Your timing for our lives. In Jesus' name, amen.

TAKE-HOME PAGE

Give each child a Take-Home page to take home. Encourage kids to select one of the six challenges for the week ahead.

PRACTICING TRUST

Keep growing in your faith and character. Choose one of the following challenges to do this week to show you trust God's timing.

CHALLENGE 1

Think of something that you're looking forward to, and brainstorm a way you can serve God until then, just as David served God by serving King Saul. For example, you could sing a song for a parent or play with a younger brother or sister. Do what you came up with as you're waiting, and thank God for His perfect timing.

CHALLENGE 2

With a parent, find pictures in a book or on the Internet that show how babies grow before they're born. Notice how perfectly God times the development of all of a baby's body parts. Talk with your parent about how God's timing is perfect even before we're born!

CHALLENGE 3

Sit down with an adult and list the things a child has to learn before being considered an adult. Then thank God for His perfect timing in the way you grow up.

CHALLENGE 4

Put a note by your alarm clock that says "Trust God's timing." Whenever you see it, say a one-sentence prayer asking God to help you follow His timing instead of your own.

CHALLENGE 5

Make a list of things you have a hard time waiting for. Show your list to a friend, and explain what you learned this week about trusting God's timing.

CHALLENGE 6

Think of someone who God has put in authority over you. Find a way to secretly serve that person. For example, you could leave a secret encouragement note or make a special snack for the person.

LESSON 4 — WE TRUST GOD'S TIMING

WE SHOW GOD'S LOVE
BY BEING HONEST

HONESTY IS...
telling the truth.

*Genesis 27:1-45:
Jacob Steals His
Brother's Blessing*

Jacob stole his brother's blessing by tricking his father into thinking Jacob was his brother, Esau. When we lie, we aren't being loving toward others. God wants us to love one another, and we show God's love by being honest. Honesty is telling the truth. Use this lesson to help children grow in honesty.

WHAT KIDS DO	WHAT YOU'LL NEED
God Sightings *(5 minutes)* Share ways they've seen God at work.	
Bible Experience *(10 minutes)* See if they can spot changes in each other and talk about honesty.	• Bible
House of Cards *(10 minutes)* Build a wall with cards and think about how honesty helps hold up relationships.	• decks of cards • tennis balls
Seeing Clearly *(10 minutes)* Look through waxed paper and consider what it means to be transparent.	• Bible • waxed paper • tape • sheet of paper • pencil
Wait 'Til You've Heard This! *(10 minutes)* Compare two versions of a story.	• a copy of *The True Story of the Three Little Pigs!* by Jon Scieszka *(from your local library)*
Life Application *(15 minutes)* Participate in a skit about some dogs that learn a valuable lesson.	• copies of the skit *(found at the end of this lesson)*

*Photocopy the Take-Home page at the end of this lesson for each child.

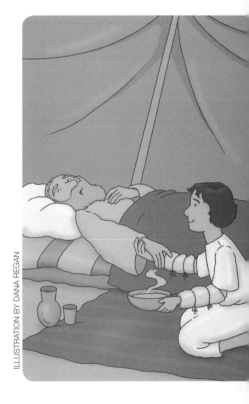

ILLUSTRATION BY DANA REGAN

HONESTY DEVOTION

Constant strife between siblings is enough to break a relationship, but dishonesty is the easiest way to break the trust of brothers and sisters. Even though God eventually worked Jacob and Esau's situation out for good (Genesis 33), God makes it clear in His Word that He detests lies (Proverbs 12:22). It's of utmost importance to be honest with our siblings and friends at all times and to not attempt to deceive them in our pursuit of selfish goals. Let kids know that being honest is one of the best things they can do to get along with others.

BIBLE FOUNDATION FOR TEACHERS

Genesis 27:1-45: Jacob Steals His Brother's Blessing

SIBLING RIVALRY

Jacob and Esau were the twin sons of Isaac and Rebekah. Even though they were essentially the same age, Esau, who was born first, still carried the traditional rights of the oldest son. These rights included becoming the head of the entire household and taking on the role of patriarch. However, before their birth, God told Rebekah that the firstborn son, Esau, would eventually serve his younger brother, Jacob (Genesis 25:23).

ISAAC WANTS TO BLESS ESAU

Isaac was getting old, and he knew that before he died he needed to bless Esau as the older son. Isaac asked Esau to hunt for some meat and prepare his favorite meal, so he could bless Esau and officially give him the right to become the head of the household. Rebekah overheard this and decided she wanted Jacob to receive this blessing.

REBEKAH'S PLOT

The Bible states, "Isaac loved Esau...but Rebekah loved Jacob" (Genesis 25:28). This may have been Rebekah's motivation for helping Jacob obtain the blessing for himself. However, it may also have been a result of Rebekah's lack of faith in God to carry out His plan of allowing Jacob to rule over his brother. In either case, Rebekah helped Jacob prepare a meal and disguise himself as Esau so the blind Isaac wouldn't recognize him. She prompted Jacob to serve his father food so he could secure the blessing of the firstborn for himself.

ILLUSTRATION BY RONNIE ROONEY

JACOB STEALS THE BLESSING

It's unclear how Isaac was so easily tricked into thinking Jacob was his favorite son, Esau. But he was successfully deceived, and Isaac ate the meal and unwittingly gave the blessing to his youngest son. Immediately after, Esau returned from hunting to find that his blessing had already been taken. He was angry with Jacob for this treachery and vowed to kill him when Isaac died. Rebekah heard about Esau's plans and decided it was necessary to send Jacob away to preserve his life.

THE RESULTS

This act of dishonesty resulted in a destroyed relationship between two brothers. It's interesting to think how differently the situation might have turned out if Rebekah and Jacob had simply trusted God to carry out His plan, instead of taking matters into their own hands.

GOD SIGHTINGS

THE LESSON

As a group, share God Sightings—ways you've seen God at work. Then celebrate how God is at work in your lives through a prayer of thanksgiving.

BIBLE EXPERIENCE

Read aloud Genesis 27:1-45.

Talk about: **God wants us to be honest with one another in everything we do. Honesty is telling the truth. ● We show God's love by being honest. Honesty is a great way to avoid problems in our families.**

Have kids stand and face a partner. Say: **Look carefully at your partner. Notice everything you can—what his or her clothes look like, any jewelry, hairstyle, and so on.** Give kids one minute. Then have partners turn their backs to each other.

Say: **Let's see how well you can spot a change in your partner. Stay facing away from each other and change at least three things about your appearance. For example, untie a shoe, roll up a pant leg, or take off your glasses.**

YOU'LL NEED:

✓ **Bible**

After everyone has made the changes, say: **When Jacob went in to receive Esau's blessing, Isaac wasn't sure he was really Esau. So Isaac asked, but Jacob lied and said he was Esau.**

Have kids turn back around to face each other. Say: **See if you can figure out what your partner changed about him- or herself.**

Afterward, lead this discussion: **How were the changes you made like or unlike the changes Jacob made to fool his father? Tell about a time you tried to trick a person into thinking you were something you weren't. What consequences could come from tricking someone?**

Talk about: **When you were changing things about yourself, you were doing it for fun, and your partner knew you were trying to be tricky. Isaac didn't know his son was trying to fool him. Jacob's dishonesty caused his family pain. Unlike Jacob, ● we show God's love by being honest.**

HOUSE OF CARDS

Say: **Jacob stole his brother's blessing by tricking his father into thinking Jacob was his brother, Esau. When we lie, we aren't being loving toward others. God wants us to love one another, and ● we show God's love by being honest.**

Talk about: **Think of a time someone tricked you. How did that make you feel? How did it affect your relationship with that person?**

Have kids form pairs, and give each pair a stack of playing cards and challenge them to build a wall together with their cards.

Then have pairs each place a tennis ball (or similar object) on the top of their card structures.

Lead this discussion: **Did your wall have integrity—did it hold up? Why or why not? The ball represents a big whopper of a lie. What happens to the integrity of your relationships when people lie to one another? Do your relationships hold up when people lie?**

Say: **To work, a wall has to have integrity—that means it has to be solid, well-built, and can't have any weak spots. We're like that, too. God can help us be strong without weak spots. If we aren't, then even little lies can get through! When we're solid and well-built, without weak spots, we tell the truth about everything—and keep out the lies. Because we love God,**  **we show God's love by being honest.**

SEEING CLEARLY

See the Teacher Prep box in advance of this activity.

Say: **Think about a time you lied to get what you wanted. You won't have to tell us about it if you don't want to; just think about it and be honest with yourself.** Allow 30 seconds for silent reflection.

Now think about the person or people you lied to. How do you think it made those people feel? Allow another 30 seconds for silent reflection. Then ask if anyone would like to share a story.

Read John 15:12. Talk about: **How does being honest fulfill this command? How does it affect your relationship when you find out a friend has been dishonest with you?**

Give everyone a long sheet of waxed paper and demonstrate how to fold it to create a blindfold. Tape the ends of the blindfold together for each child. Say: **Look through the blindfold. Imagine you had to spend a day looking through one of these. What would that be like?**

Have kids each try to read the sentence you wrote before class while wearing the waxy blindfold. Once everyone's had a turn, have them take off their blindfolds and read it.

Lead this discussion: **What does it mean to be transparent? How is reading without a blindfold like or unlike being transparent and honest in your relationships? What can you do to be more transparent, or clear, in your relationships?**

YOU'LL NEED:

✓ **Bible**
✓ **waxed paper**
✓ **tape**
✓ **sheet of paper**
✓ **pencil**

TEACHER PREP

Children will need a long sheet of waxed paper to use as a blindfold. Fasten blindfolds with tape, or have children hold the waxed paper to their eyes.

In advance, write this sentence in small letters on a sheet of paper:

"No one wants to be a liar, liar pants on fire."

Say: **It was hard to see clearly through the wax paper blindfold. Our relationships are like that—when we aren't transparent or completely honest, it makes it hard for our relationships to work. Jacob wasn't very transparent with his dad. Just like Jacob hurt his family when he tricked his father, we hurt each other when we aren't transparent.**

Think of how you feel when someone isn't honest with you to help you remember ● we show God's love by being honest.

WAIT 'TIL YOU'VE HEARD THIS!

Have kids get into pairs and tell each other the story of the three little pigs from memory.

Then read *The True Story of the Three Little Pigs!* aloud.

Compare the two versions of the same story. Talk about why it's important to be honest about things that happen.

LIFE APPLICATION

Say: **Today we're learning how ● we show God's love by being honest. Let's participate in a skit about some dogs that learn a valuable lesson.**

Explain that the people who don't have a part in the skit are the audience. The audience will have the part of being dogs at the dog park. Have them practice acting like dogs by barking, panting, and sitting like dogs.

Have two kids act out the skit "No Bones About It—A Dog's Tale," found at the end of this lesson.

Afterward, lead this discussion: **Why was being honest the right choice in this skit? Tell about a time you or someone else took something without asking. Why is telling the truth a loving choice?**

YOU'LL NEED:

✓ **a copy of *The True Story of the Three Little Pigs!* by Jon Scieszka (from your local library)**

YOU'LL NEED:

✓ **copies of the skit (found at the end of this lesson)**

TEACHER TIP

Kids can get into character by making dog-eared hats with socks or strips of paper attached to any type of hat.

Talk about: **Even though Kibbles was tempted to blame someone else for taking the bone, he made the right choice by being honest with his friend Bow-Wowser. It's not always easy being honest, but when we're honest with each other we're showing each other love. Being honest with one another keeps us out of trouble. Or as Bow-Wowser would say—being honest keeps us "out of the doghouse."** ● **We show God's love by being honest.**

PRAYER

Dear God, thank You for loving us so much. Please help us show others Your love through our honesty. Thank You for being with us. In Jesus' name, amen.

TAKE-HOME PAGE

Give each child a Take-Home page to take home. Encourage kids to select one of the six challenges for the week ahead.

PRACTICING HONESTY

Keep growing in your faith and character. Choose one of the following challenges to do this week to show God's love by being honest.

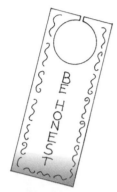

CHALLENGE 1

Make a door hanger for your bedroom door that says "Be honest" to remind you that we show God's love to our brothers, sisters, and friends by being honest.

CHALLENGE 2

We speak honesty with our tongues. For a fun reminder of this, hold your tongue with your fingers while telling your family we show God's love by being honest. Keep saying it until you can stop laughing and they can understand you!

CHALLENGE 3

Be honest with your parents about the way you treat your brothers, sisters, and friends. Before you go to bed, tell your parents how you treated each person you were around that day.

CHALLENGE 4

Choose an honest character from one of your favorite books. In a notebook or journal, write a list of ways that character shows love through honesty.

CHALLENGE 5

Gather a bag of unusual or pretty pebbles and clean them. Get a jar and tape a piece of paper to it that says "Love Honestly." Every time you choose to show love to someone by being honest, place one of your rocks in the jar. See how quickly your jar fills up!

CHALLENGE 6

Fill two small glasses with milk. Stir a spoonful of lemon juice into one glass. Wait a minute, and then have a family member or friend taste the lemon milk. Explain that a little bit of lemon juice ruined the milk, just like a little lie can really mess up a relationship. Share the good milk.

NO BONES ABOUT IT—A DOG'S TALE

This dog tale teaches kids about telling the truth.

The scene opens as Kibbles and Bow-Wowser enter the dog park. Kibbles pants and prances, friskier than Bow-Wowser, who scratches his head and seems to be searching the ground.

KIBBLES

Hey, Bow-Wowser, whatcha doin'?

BOW-WOWSER

Oh, hi there, Kibbles. I'm looking for something...

KIBBLES

(Panting) Hey, you can look later—let's go chase some cars! *(Looks to audience.)* Bark if you want to join us!

BOW-WOWSER

You all go ahead and chase cars if you like. You know, at my age, I only chase parked cars. *(Continues to look around, scratching head, searching the ground.)*

KIBBLES

Aw, come on, Bow-Wowser—you're not that old.

BOW-WOWSER

Some days I can be pretty forgetful...I'd forget my name if I didn't have my collar I.D. *(Points at the base of his neck.)*

(Continues searching.) Now, where did I put that...?

KIBBLES

Put what? What did ya lose, Bow-Wowser?

BOW-WOWSER

A nice big bone—I buried it here somewhere yesterday, and now I can't find it. *(Looks to audience.)* Pant if you love bones! *(Allows time.)* Do you all know where it is?

KIBBLES

Um, a bone? *(Looking a bit distressed)* Woof!

BOW-WOWSER

Hush, puppy! I'm thinking! Now where did I put that bone? Say, maybe you all can help me find it—weren't you all here yesterday when I buried that bone? *(Looks to audience.)* Bark if you were here at the dog park playing yesterday.

KIBBLES

Woof! Um, uh...you mean the um, big, chewy, delicious bone... *(licking lips)* um, you buried yesterday?

BOW-WOWSER

Exactly! Say, Kibbles, you didn't happen to see any of these dogs take it, did you? *(Gestures to audience.)*

KIBBLES

No, they wouldn't do that, right? *(Looks to audience.)* Pant if you're innocent! *(Allows time.)* But, um, uh...a certain Dalmatian was spotted in the area.

BOW-WOWSER

Dalmatian—spotted! *(Laughs/barks.)* Oh, that's a good one! Thanks for trying to cheer me up—but I'd be a lot happier if I could find that bone! *(Looks to audience.)* Can you all help me look? Bark if you'll help me. *(Allows time.)* Okay, let's go!

KIBBLES

(Allows time for kids to start looking.) Wait! Wait! All dogs, listen. Sit, doggies, sit! *(Waits for audience to sit.)* Um, Bow-Wowser, I, um...I need to be honest with you, and with all of you. *(Looks to audience.)* I took the bone.

BOW-WOWSER

Thank goodness! *(Looks to audience.)* Cheer and bark with me, doggies! *(Allows time.)*

KIBBLES

You're glad I took the bone?

BOW-WOWSER

Don't be r-r-r-idiculous! I'm just thankful that my memory and sense of smell aren't as bad as I thought!

KIBBLES

(Looking sad, pouting) Then you are upset with me for taking the bone...

BOW-WOWSER

Oh, there'll be other bones—I'm just glad you decided to be honest with me about taking it.

KIBBLES

I guess when you really care about someone, you want to be honest with them, huh, Bow-Wowser?

BOW-WOWSER

Being honest is the best thing if you want to stay out of the doghouse with me... *(Looks to audience.)* That's something we can all cheer about. Bark with me!

KIBBLES

From now on this pup is going to be upfront and honest with everyone!

BOW-WOWSER

Now it's my turn to be honest. *(Looks and points off to the side.)* It's been a few years, but that bowl of puppy chow over on your back porch sure looks tasty. Do you suppose we could "paws" *(holds up hands)* and take a quick snack break?

KIBBLES

(Panting) You got it, Bow-Wowser! Then you can show me how to chase those parked cars!

WE TELL THE TRUTH

HONESTY IS...
telling the truth.

Proverbs 11:3; 23:19;
26:18-19:
God Loves Honesty

The book of Proverbs makes it clear that honesty guides us in life. There are many proverbs in this book that describe what an honest and dishonest person look like—and how they act. Use this lesson to help children learn to do the right thing and tell the truth.

WHAT KIDS DO	WHAT YOU'LL NEED
God Sightings *(5 minutes)* Share ways they've seen God at work.	
Bible Experience *(10 minutes)* Move closer together as they share truths, and pull apart as they say untruths.	• Bible
Draw on the Truth *(15 minutes)* Create a cartoon while considering that lying is no laughing matter.	• Bibles • pencils • copies of the handout *(found at the end of this lesson)*
Act on the Truth *(10 minutes)* Consider honest and dishonest responses and if there's a difference between big and small lies.	• Bible • pencils • handouts from previous activity
Truth Telling *(10 minutes)* Discuss and role-play situations in which they might be tempted to lie.	
Life Application *(10 minutes)* Hide objects in clay sculptures and discuss how hiding the truth is the same as lying.	• modeling dough or clay

ILLUSTRATION BY RONNIE ROONEY

Photocopy the Take-Home page at the end of this lesson for each child.

53

HONESTY DEVOTION

This week, as you encounter an honest truth, such as a sincere compliment, be open to what truth God might be sharing with you through it. What does God have for you to learn or discover about yourself? about others? or about Him? Pray that kids will choose not to lie to others, to themselves, or to God.

BIBLE FOUNDATION FOR TEACHERS

Proverbs 11:3; 23:19; 26:18-19: God Loves Honesty

WHAT THE BIBLE SAYS

Solomon says those who are honest—those who do what's right in all situations, even when nobody's watching—discover that their honesty guides them in life. They know and do the truth. The truth lasts forever, but lies are revealed early on. Solomon describes someone who deceives his friend and then claims he was just joking as a dangerous man. It's as if he is shooting a deadly weapon—his duplicity has great power to do harm.

WHAT IT MEANS

For all his wisdom, Solomon wasn't perfect. He built temples dedicated to his wives' pagan gods. He disobeyed direct orders from God to not multiply wives, horses, or gold as he sank into idolatry. This was a wise man? Yes. Wise...imperfect...and truthful. Solomon saw with great clarity the power of untruth and how powerful truth was in his own life and the lives of others. Solomon knew leading a dishonest life destroys a person.

WHY IT MATTERS

White lies. Insincere compliments. A flattering comment that overstates how well that new hairdo really frames a friend's face. What's the harm? There's damage, even if it's not immediately evident.

First, there's damage to the relationship when the person on the receiving end senses the insincerity. When someone identifies a liar, trust evaporates. Relationships are strained or broken. Second, there's damage to the liar. A compromised life is hard to live. And finally, there's damage to the liar's relationship with God. It's as important to seek forgiveness for a white lie as for any other sort of lie.

ILLUSTRATION BY DREW ROSE

GOD SIGHTINGS

As a group, share God Sightings—ways you've seen God at work. Then celebrate how God is at work in your lives through a prayer of thanksgiving.

BIBLE EXPERIENCE

One at a time read the following verses: Proverbs 11:3; Proverbs 12:19; and Proverbs 26:18-19. Each time, ask kids what the Scripture says about honesty.

Talk about: **Today we're learning what the Bible says about honesty. Honesty is telling the truth.**

Have kids spread out around the room.

Say: **Lying pulls apart our relationships with each other and with God. But honesty brings us together. Let's see what that's like.**

Start by telling truths about yourself, such as "I like football" or "I play the piano." Each time you share, take a step closer to someone else. Then have another person do the same thing. Have kids take turns sharing truths until everyone is close enough to link arms in a circle.

Say: **Now we're going to take turns saying things that aren't true. You can say something about yourself that's not true or make up something that we all know is not true, such as "the sky is green."**

Each time someone shares an untruth, have him or her take a small step away from the group while keeping arms linked. Keep going until there's no option but to let go of the links.

Lead this discussion: **How do lies separate us from each other? How do lies separate us from God? Tell about a time someone lied to you. What happened to your friendship?**

Talk about: **Lying destroys relationships. Just one lie can cause someone to lose trust and even lose a friend. That's why we tell the truth. Sometimes telling the truth can be**

YOU'LL NEED:

✓ **Bible**

difficult, but maintaining honesty keeps us close to God and others.

YOU'LL NEED:

✓ Bibles

✓ pencils

✓ copies of the handout *(found at the end of this lesson)*

DRAW ON THE TRUTH

Say: **In the book of Proverbs, Solomon says those who are honest—those who do what's right in all situations, even when nobody's watching—discover that their honesty guides them in life. They know and do the truth.**

Knock, Knock jokes can be funny, but Proverbs 26:18-19 says that lying is no joke. In fact, it's as serious as shooting arrows of death! On your handouts, create a cartoon to help you remember this important truth. First, let's read a few more words from the Bible about telling the truth to help with the cartoons.

Have volunteers read aloud Proverbs 11:3, Proverbs 12:19, and Proverbs 26:18-19.

Allow time for kids to fill in the cartoons on their handouts. Have older kids help younger ones, if necessary. Invite kids to share their finished work.

Then lead this discussion: **What good things can come out of telling the truth? Why do kids sometimes lie to their parents? What advice would you give a child your age about telling the truth?**

Say: **Lying is no joking matter. God tells us to tell the truth all the time. God loves honesty, so ● we tell the truth.**

ACT ON THE TRUTH

YOU'LL NEED:

✓ Bible

✓ pencils

✓ handouts from previous activity

Say: **God loves honesty. And for good reason. Can you imagine what it would be like to live in a dishonest world where you couldn't trust anyone? Imagine what it would be like if everything anyone said was a lie. Let's pretend that's how it is for a few minutes.**

Direct kids to the bottom of their handouts. Say: **Think about each of these situations and write what the people would do in a dishonest world.** Kids can work alone or in pairs.

Allow several minutes for kids to write. Ask for volunteers to share their responses. Then lead this discussion: **What are some better ways to handle these situations? Tell about a situation you faced where being honest was really hard. Explain whether there's a difference between big lies and little lies. Why is honesty important?**

Say: **Honesty can be tough, especially when the truth is going to get us into trouble. But**  **we tell the truth no matter what. All lies come out eventually, so it's best to start with the truth.**

TRUTH TELLING

Discuss the following situations where people might normally be tempted to lie. Have kids take turns role-playing each scenario in pairs to show how they might respond truthfully in that situation.

- **You break your mom's favorite bottle of perfume and she asks if you know who did it.**

- **A friend just got a new haircut that you don't like. Your friend wants to know what you think of the new look.**

- **Your aunt gave you an outfit for your birthday that isn't your style at all.**

- **You didn't finish your homework because you were watching TV.**

Lead this discussion: **What are other times you might be tempted to lie? What did you learn from these scenarios that might help you tell the truth in the future?**

LIFE APPLICATION

Give each child a piece of modeling clay. Have kids find a small object in the room that they can place inside their clay, but don't let kids show each other their items. Then have kids sculpt something totally different from their object with their clay, with the real object hidden inside.

Allow time, and then have kids take turns showing their sculptures to others. Kids will guess what's inside the sculpture based on what they can see. After everyone has shown his

YOU'LL NEED:

✓ **modeling dough or clay**

or her sculpture, have all the kids open theirs up to reveal the hidden object.

Lead this discussion: **What was it like trying to guess the hidden objects? How is hiding the truth like or unlike lying? Tell about a time someone hid the truth so well you had no idea it was a lie for a while.**

Talk about: **Honesty is more than just not lying. It means telling the whole truth. When we hide the truth, that's the same thing as lying, and it can have the same negative effects. ● We tell the truth, and we don't hide it.**

PRAYER
God, thank You that You never lie. Even when it's tough, please help us to tell the truth always—just like You. In Jesus' name, amen.

TAKE-HOME PAGE

Give each child a Take-Home page to take home. Encourage kids to select one of the six challenges for the week ahead.

PRACTICING HONESTY

Keep growing in your faith and character. Choose one of the following challenges to do this week to tell the truth.

CHALLENGE 1
Choose one of the proverbs we discussed as a group: Proverbs 11:3, Proverbs 12:19, or Proverbs 26:18-19. Write one on a sheet of paper and post it in your bedroom to remember what God says about honesty.

CHALLENGE 2
Play a game with a younger sibling and explain why it's important to follow the rules. Tell your sibling that not cheating is being honest.

CHALLENGE 3
Drink a crystal clear glass of water as you remember that God is completely honest. He never lies. Thank God for being trustworthy.

CHALLENGE 4
Write your own proverbs about telling the truth in a notebook or journal. Then share them with your family.

CHALLENGE 5
Look up the word *tact* in a dictionary. Talk with your parents about the difference between tact and complete honesty.

CHALLENGE 6
Ask God to show you something that you need to be honest about. Perhaps you've told a lie or hidden the truth. Ask God to help you tell the truth in that area.

DRAW ON THE TRUTH

Knock, Knock

(Who's there?)

Otis!

(Otis who?)

Otis a sin to
tell a lie!

ILLUSTRATION BY PATRICK CREYTS

SITUATION 1:

While at the park,
Melanie and Sasha
found a wallet with
$100 in cash.

_____
_____
_____
_____
_____
_____
_____

SITUATION 2:

People are passing the
offering plate at church.
Alex only has $5, and
he's meeting friends at
the mall later. He had
his eye on something
that's $20.

_____
_____
_____
_____
_____
_____

SITUATION 3:

Chris spent a lot of time
studying for a test, and
he felt prepared. But
one of the questions
has him stumped.

_____
_____
_____
_____
_____
_____

WE TELL THE TRUTH NO MATTER WHAT

HONESTY IS...
telling the truth.

Mark 14:53-65:
People Lie About Jesus

Soldiers arrested Jesus and took Him to the high priest's home. Many people falsely accused Jesus, yet He remained silent. Finally, the high priest asked Jesus if He was the Messiah. Jesus answered truthfully that He was the Son of God, so soldiers beat Him and led Him away to be crucified. Jesus knew the consequences of telling the truth, but He refused to lie. Use this lesson to help children learn that like Jesus, we tell the truth no matter what.

WHAT KIDS DO	WHAT YOU'LL NEED
God Sightings *(5 minutes)* Share ways they've seen God at work.	
Bible Experience *(10 minutes)* Tell a story to learn the destructive power of lies.	• Bible
Poking Holes *(10 minutes)* Discover how poking holes in the truth ruins things.	• plastic foam cup • large nail • sink
Truth Plants *(15 minutes)* Create a plant to help them remember to always tell the truth.	• construction paper • straws • scissors • markers • glue or tape • cups with rocks
Aim for Truth *(10 minutes)* Compare "golfing" to telling the truth.	• Bible • cotton balls • pencils
Life Application *(10 minutes)* Watch a video about cheating and telling the truth.	• *Character by God's Design* DVD • DVD player

ILLUSTRATION BY DANA REGAN

*Photocopy the Take-Home page at the end of this lesson for each child.

HONESTY DEVOTION

Jesus suffered for telling the truth, but ultimately we know that truth led to victory and freedom from sin. Speaking of Himself and His relationship with God, Jesus said, "A person who seeks to honor the one who sent him speaks truth, not lies" (John 7:18). We honor God, the one who sends us, by speaking truth. Think of moments it might be easier to lie—when a child asks a question you don't know how to answer, when someone asks how you're doing on a bad day, when you've made an embarrassing mistake—and challenge yourself to tell the truth instead, no matter the consequences.

BIBLE FOUNDATION FOR TEACHERS

Mark 14:53-65: People Lie About Jesus

SEARCHING FOR LIES

Jesus' sentence of death was imminent—but the religious leaders needed to come up with a crime to fit the punishment that was in store. The only problem? No one could find any wrongdoing by the defendant. So to get the job done, the religious leaders resorted to lies. Accusers drummed up false witnesses and made up testimony, but even then, their witnesses "contradicted each other" and "didn't get their stories straight." In this dishonest approach to criminal proceedings, the truth was an afterthought—at best.

ILLUSTRATION BY DANA REGAN

CASE CLOSED

With false testimony hanging in the air like smoke from a grease fire, the high priest challenged Jesus to defend Himself. "What do you have to say for yourself?" he demanded. Jesus remained silent. In the style of a lead prosecuting attorney, the high priest changed his line of questioning: "Are you the Messiah, the Son of the Blessed One?" It's a question Jesus couldn't leave unanswered. To remain silent would have been the same as lying. "I Am," Jesus said.

The room erupted at this blasphemous admission, and the high priest, who otherwise might have tried to restore order, tore his clothes in horror and called for an end to the trial. "Why do we need other witnesses? What is your verdict?" No deliberations were even necessary. Jesus was declared guilty and condemned to death. Lies couldn't convict Him. Truth, from the One who is truth (John 14:6), was the only evidence the religious leaders needed to condemn Jesus to death.

TRUTH AND CONSEQUENCES

Earlier in His ministry, Jesus said this about truth: "And you will know the truth, and the truth will set you free" (John 8:32). The leading priests heard the truth about Jesus, but they didn't set Him free. Instead, they spit at Him, called Him names, hit His blindfolded face, and jeered. They continued with their plan to put Him to death. Truth, it seemed, caused Jesus more trouble than a lie would have.

THE LESSON

GOD SIGHTINGS

As a group, share God Sightings—ways you've seen God at work. Then celebrate how God is at work in your lives through a prayer of thanksgiving.

BIBLE EXPERIENCE

Talk about: **God gave us the Ten Commandments so we would know ways to honor Him. One of those ways is to tell the truth—all the time.** ● **We tell the truth no matter what because it honors God and shows Him we love Him, too.**

Read Mark 14:53-54. Have kids stand in a circle.

Read Mark 14:55-59. Talk about: **People lied about Jesus. I'm going to start a story. "One-up" each other to make the story into a "whopper." For example, if I say, "The Bible says Jesus could fly," someone might say, "The Bible says Jesus could fly as fast as a supersonic jet."** Explain that when someone adds a "whopper," he or she must take a step back from the circle. Use the starters in the Teacher Tip box, or create your own!

YOU'LL NEED:

✓ **Bible**

TEACHER TIP

Some possible whopper starters:

- The Bible says Jesus had laser vision.

- The Bible says Jesus could jump higher than a building.

- The Bible says Jesus could shrink Himself down to the size of an ant.

After one round, read Mark 14:60-62. Then say: **Time to flip the whopper. This time you are to tell nothing but the truth. Your last whopper starter is this: "Jesus is the Son of God, and here's why."**

Allow one minute. If kids can't come up with something right away, they can say "skip."

Say: **After Jesus said who He really was, this is what happened.** Read Mark 14:63-65. Then talk about: **Jesus told the truth...even though He knew it would get Him in trouble.**

Lead this discussion: **Why do you think Jesus told the truth? Tell about a time you told the truth and got in trouble. Why do you think God wants us to always tell the truth?**

Talk about: **Our God is a God of truth. That's why one of the Ten Commandments is about telling the truth—all the time. When we lie, we move further away from living as God wants us to live. That's one reason ● we tell the truth no matter what, just as Jesus did. He told the truth, even if it meant He'd get in trouble. Let's decide today that telling the truth is the right thing to do.**

POKING HOLES

Have everyone sit in a circle.

Explain that you're going to illustrate what happens when people lie.

Say: **I need everyone to think of lies they've heard. In a minute, I'll ask you to call them out.**

Next, place a cup upside down on the table, and every time someone names a lie, poke the nail through the bottom and the sides of the cup.

Remove the nail each time, but keep poking until the cup has several holes.

Hold the cup over a sink and pour in water.

Discuss how lies can ruin the way things were meant to be.

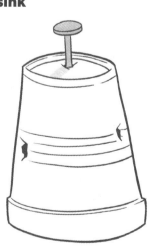

YOU'LL NEED:

✓ **plastic foam cup**
✓ **large nail**
✓ **sink**

TRUTH PLANTS

YOU'LL NEED:

✓ **construction paper**

✓ **straws**

✓ **scissors**

✓ **markers**

✓ **glue or tape**

✓ **cups with rocks**

Say: **The ancient Jewish leaders couldn't find a reason to put Jesus to death, so they made up lies about Him. Jesus remained silent until they asked if He was the Messiah, the Son of the Blessed One. Even though He knew it would get Him in trouble, Jesus answered truthfully, "I Am." Like Him,**  **we can always tell the truth no matter what.**

Have kids form pairs and discuss the following questions. Read a question, allow time for kids to share, and then read the next question.

- **Tell about a time it was hard for you to tell the truth.**

- **Tell about a time in the future that it might be hard to tell the truth.**

- **Why is it important to tell the truth no matter what?**

Next, set out supplies and show kids how to make a "Truth Plant" with construction paper by cutting out several leaves and a center circle with petals. Use a straw as a stem.

On one leaf or flower petal write "Tell the truth." Then write "no matter what!" on another leaf or flower petal. Write those two phrases on all the leaves or flower petals, and put together the Truth Plant with glue or tape.

Place it in a cup of small rocks (or marbles) so it stands up.

Say: **Jesus told the truth even when it was hard to do. We can always tell the truth, too, just as He did. We tell the truth no matter what.**

AIM FOR TRUTH

YOU'LL NEED:

✓ **Bible**

✓ **cotton balls**

✓ **pencils**

Read Deuteronomy 5:32. Ask: **What does this verse have to do with telling the truth no matter what?**

Have children try this activity: Use a pencil as a golf club to hit a cotton ball like a golf ball. The goal is to hit the cotton ball to a specific point across the room. Once you've done this, do it again to see if you can accomplish the goal with fewer strokes.

Lead this discussion: **What was challenging about this game? What kinds of things did you do to aim your ball? What can make it challenging to tell the truth no matter what?**

How does keeping your eye on God help you tell the truth no matter what? Why is it important to tell the truth no matter what?

Ask everyone to reflect silently on this last question: **What's one area in your life where you need to commit to being more truthful, no matter what the consequences are?**

Say: **Jesus chose to tell the truth even though He knew He'd be put to death for it. He knew that telling the truth honors God. Like Jesus,** **we tell the truth no matter what the consequences.**

LIFE APPLICATION

Talk about: **When you're playing a game, it's best to follow the rules. When you break the rules of a game just to win, that's called...**gesture to kids to answer all at once**...cheating. Exactly. Let's join a game already in progress, and watch a heated battle for the world mini-golf championship—the Mini-Masters.**

Play "The Mini-Masters" (track 4) on the *Character by God's Design* DVD.

Afterward, lead this discussion: **What do you think about Dylan's choice? Explain what's worse: cheating to win and getting away with it, or telling the truth and losing the game. Talk about whether it's easy or hard to tell the truth—even when no one can see you cheat just a little.**

Say: **Dylan was faced with a choice: cheat and get away with it, or tell the truth and possibly lose the whole championship. God loves the truth, and He wants us to tell the truth all the time—even if it means owning up to something we did wrong. Just as Dylan did,** **we tell the truth no matter what. The truth is better than a trophy!**

PRAYER
God, please help us follow Jesus' example and be truthful no matter what. In Jesus' name, amen.

TAKE-HOME PAGE

Give each child a Take-Home page to take home. Encourage kids to select one of the six challenges for the week ahead.

PRACTICING HONESTY

Keep growing in your faith and character. Choose one of the following challenges to do this week to tell the truth no matter what.

CHALLENGE 1

Sometimes a lie can grow because we don't come clean and tell the truth no matter what. Ask God to show you if there's a lie you need to tell the truth about. Then do it with His help.

CHALLENGE 2

Read this week's Bible passage, Mark 14:53-65, with a parent. Think about what would've happened if no one lied. Then retell what happened together with everyone telling the truth. Talk about how telling the truth or lying affects others.

CHALLENGE 3

Think about a lie you've told recently to avoid getting into trouble. Ask God to give you the strength to tell the truth about that situation; then go and talk to the person about what really happened.

CHALLENGE 4

Create a short chant similar to "Liar, liar pants on fire" as a reminder to tell the truth. For example, you might come up with something like: "Tell the truth (pause) no matter what—or just keep (pause) your mouth shut." Every time you're tempted to lie, repeat the chant in your head.

CHALLENGE 5

Read Acts 5:1-11 to discover what happened to two people who chose to lie rather than tell the truth about what they had done. Each time you wash your hands this week, commit to coming clean and always telling the truth no matter what the consequences might be.

CHALLENGE 6

Do words come in flavors? Ask a parent if you can taste baking chocolate. Then try milk chocolate. Think about which one tastes better. How would lies taste if they were a flavor? How about the truth? Think about which one you want coming from your mouth.

THE HOLY SPIRIT GUIDES US

HONESTY IS...
telling the truth.

Galatians 5:13-17:
Paul Tells Christians to
Do What's Right

Paul wrote to the Galatians to remind them to be careful that they don't use their freedom to do wrong things. He wanted them to remember that we're called to serve one another in love. His words remind us that when we're following God, we can do the right thing. Paul also said that when we let the Holy Spirit guide our lives, we'll desire to serve others in love. Use this lesson to help children learn to allow the Holy Spirit to guide them to serve one another through honesty.

WHAT KIDS DO	WHAT YOU'LL NEED
God Sightings *(5 minutes)* Share ways they've seen God at work.	
Bible Experience *(10 minutes)* Explore choices they can make alone or with the Holy Spirit.	• Bible • poster board • markers
Follow the Recipe *(10 minutes)* Explore a connection between following a recipe and following the Holy Spirit.	• copies of the handout *(found at the end of this lesson)* • pencils
Law of the Land *(15 minutes)* Create rules for their own land, and connect that to how the Holy Spirit leads us.	• Bible • handouts from the previous activity • pencils
Cook It Up! *(10 minutes)* Follow a recipe for a snack together.	• simple recipe • ingredients for the recipe • paper plates and napkins
Life Application *(10 minutes)* Follow the leader.	

ILLUSTRATION BY RONNIE ROONEY

Photocopy the Take-Home page at the end of this lesson for each child.

HONESTY DEVOTION

Being guided by the Holy Spirit isn't always an easy choice, but it's always a better choice. Be brutally honest with yourself for a moment: Have you been faced with these kinds of choices? Lashing out in anger, as opposed to responding in love? Knee-jerk reacting to a crisis, instead of choosing eye-of-the-storm peace? Honestly approach God in conversation, facing up to your sins and weaknesses—especially those you usually like to ignore. Ask the Spirit to guide you, to help you navigate life's temptation to sin. Then after your prayer, continue to rely on the Spirit, day after day, trusting in the Spirit's power instead of your own.

BIBLE FOUNDATION FOR TEACHERS

Galatians 5:13-17: Paul Tells Christians to Do What's Right

FREE TO LOVE

Paul wraps up his letter to the churches in Galatia by establishing the idea that in Christ we're set free from the Law—the Old Testament regulations for holy living. Paul wants to make sure the Galatians don't misunderstand him: Belief in Christ is not a free pass to sin. Instead, it's freedom to love. Paul reiterates the importance of what Jesus himself called one of the greatest commandments: "Love your neighbor as yourself." This all sounds rather idyllic and rosy, doesn't it? Freedom, love, everybody hugging and getting along...But, as Paul well knows, it's not quite as easy as it sounds.

SPIRIT VS. FLESH

There's a part of us called our "flesh" or our "sinful nature." Rabbis during Paul's time emphasized a split between the "good impulse" and the "bad impulse" within all human beings—the "good vs. evil" battle that wages within us all. Paul builds upon this idea in Galatians 5 when he contrasts "living by the Spirit" with living according to this sinful nature. We each deal with it. We all know, deep down, that Paul speaks the truth. No matter how much we like the tranquil picture of love, freedom, and happiness, we know that selfish sin lurks within us all, threatening to rip that picture to shreds.

ILLUSTRATION BY RONNIE ROONEY

POWER PUNCH

No matter how hard we try—no matter how much we muster up our courage and, with best intentions, battle valiantly—we simply cannot win the inner "good vs. evil" battle on our own. Paul makes it clear that no amount of human strength alone can defeat the power of our sinful nature. Only one hero can defeat the flesh: God's Holy Spirit. Paul calls the Galatians (and us) to let the Holy Spirit guide our lives. This isn't passive, as if sitting on a wagon being pulled by the Spirit; it's active. The only way to overcome "flesh" is to take action, following God's lead and enthusiastically making choices to be guided by God's Spirit.

THE LESSON

GOD SIGHTINGS

As a group, share God Sightings—ways you've seen God at work. Then celebrate how God is at work in your lives through a prayer of thanksgiving.

BIBLE EXPERIENCE

Talk about: **Knowing which way to go when we have a tough decision is sometimes hard. Thankfully, God sent us the Holy Spirit as a guide! We're sure to stay on the right path when**  **the Holy Spirit guides us.**

Have kids tell about a time they had trouble telling the truth.

Talk about: **The book of Galatians in the Bible is actually a letter Paul wrote about 2,000 years ago to the people in Galatia. They were having trouble making good choices and needed to know that ⬤ the Holy Spirit guides us in making good choices.**

Read the following situations (and feel free to add your own), and ask for kids to tell how someone might react in each situation with a lie. Write kids' responses in the first column (see the Teacher Prep box in the margin).

- **Your mother catches you with a cookie you shouldn't have.**

- **You borrow your sibling's favorite shirt and get a stain on it.**

YOU'LL NEED:

✓ **Bible**

✓ **poster board**

✓ **markers**

TEACHER PREP

Divide your poster board into two columns. Label one column "Sinful Nature" and the other "Holy Spirit."

- You get in trouble for something you did.

- Your friends are going to a movie you aren't allowed to go to.

Read Galatians 5:13-17. Then talk about: **Paul tells us we have the freedom to make choices about what we do. Love instead of hate. Be nice to people. Do what God wants. Tell the truth. Now I'll read the situations again. This time tell how the Holy Spirit might guide us.** Write answers in the second column.

Lead this discussion: **How have you reacted in similar situations? Why do you think we need the Holy Spirit to tell the truth? What can you do to let the Holy Spirit guide you to be honest?**

Talk about: **God gives us the freedom to live the way we want. But if we just follow our own desires and wants, we might make some pretty bad choices! ● The Holy Spirit guides us to do what's right.**

FOLLOW THE RECIPE

Say: **Paul wrote to the Galatians to remind them to be careful that they don't use their freedom to do wrong things. He wanted them to remember that we're called to serve one another in love. Paul also said that when we let the Holy Spirit guide us, we'll desire to do good and serve others in love.**

Read the directions on the top activity on the handout. Allow time for kids to work alone or in pairs.

Then lead this discussion: **How is following a recipe like or unlike following the Holy Spirit? What do you think it's like to be guided by the Holy Spirit to love others? Why do you think the Holy Spirit would never guide us to lie? Why is it unloving to lie to others? How can you "serve others" by being honest?**

Say: **● When the Holy Spirit guides us, we'll do right. Look for ways the Holy Spirit might want to guide you.**

LAW OF THE LAND

Talk about: **Paul told the early Christians that when we're guided by the Holy Spirit, we'll serve others in love. Tell one way you served or were served by someone this week.**

Then direct children to the "Law of the Land" activity on their handouts and read the directions. Let kids work alone or in pairs. Invite them to share their creativity when they've finished!

Lead this discussion: **Explain whether any of your rules related to honesty. How important is honesty in a society or family?** Read Galatians 5:25. **What does it mean to "live by the Spirit"? When is it easiest and hardest for you to follow the Holy Spirit's guidance?**

Say: **Choosing right from wrong can be difficult! But thankfully, we have a helper sent from God to lead us!** ● **The Holy Spirit guides us to do what's right.**

YOU'LL NEED:

✓ **Bible**

✓ **pencils**

✓ **handouts from the previous activity**

COOK IT UP!

Have kids wash their hands. Then prepare food together using a simple recipe.

As you eat the food together, lead this discussion: **How might the food have turned out if we hadn't followed the recipe's "guidance"? What does it takes to follow the Holy Spirit's guidance?**

Say: ● **The Holy Spirit guides us to do what's right.**

YOU'LL NEED:

✓ **simple recipe**

✓ **ingredients for the recipe**

✓ **paper plates and napkins**

ALLERGY ALERT

Food allergies can be dangerous and even life-threatening. Consult with parents and be aware of any allergies the kids in your group might have.

LIFE APPLICATION

Talk about: **When God created us, He gave us freedom to make choices. We can choose our friends, whether or not to listen to our parents, what to eat, and how we're going to behave. So we want to use that freedom to choose wisely!**

FOR TEACHERS:
EXPERIENTIAL LEARNING

This lesson uses Experiential Learning— learning by doing. Kids remember 90 percent more when they do something. They remember 20 percent when they only hear it and 10 percent when they read it. Here's to doing— and learning!

In Paul's letter to the Galatians, he reminded the people about letting the Holy Spirit guide them to make good choices. Let's see what that means.

Explain that you'll choose a leader to try to guide the others from where they are to a different part of your room. Have the leader decide on the pattern and number of claps he or she is going to use to guide the others, such as three quick claps or "shave and a haircut" rhythm claps.

Have kids close their eyes and follow their leader's claps. Give others a turn as leader, as time allows.

Afterward, lead this discussion: **What made it difficult to follow your leader in this game? What can make it difficult to know when the Holy Spirit is guiding you? What can you do to make it easier to follow the Holy Spirit?**

Talk about: **The Holy Spirit guides us to do what's right. Just as we had to pay attention in this game, we have to pay attention to make sure we're following the Holy Spirit. Paul wrote in Galatians 5:25, "Since we are living by the Spirit, let us follow the Spirit's leading in every part of our lives." When we listen,**  **the Holy Spirit guides us!**

PRAYER
God, thank You for giving us the Holy Spirit to guide us. Help us follow You. In Jesus' name, amen.

TAKE-HOME PAGE

Give each child a Take-Home page to take home. Encourage kids to select one of the six challenges for the week ahead.

PRACTICING HONESTY

Keep growing in your faith and character. Choose one of the following challenges to do this week to follow the Holy Spirit.

CHALLENGE 1

On a map, mark the locations of your home and three places you go often. With an adult, follow the map to those locations. Discuss how the map is a reliable travel guide, and then talk about how the Holy Spirit is a reliable life guide.

CHALLENGE 2

Use sidewalk chalk to draw pictures on the sidewalk of ways you can love and serve others. Then commit to listening to the Holy Spirit and showing love to one other person today.

CHALLENGE 3

Ask your parents for kid-appropriate magazines. Look through them to find three people you think might be worth following. Tell a parent why you chose those people, and then tell why you follow the Holy Spirit's guidance.

CHALLENGE 4

Serve a friend a healthy snack, and tell your friend how the Holy Spirit guides us to do what's right and serve others in love.

CHALLENGE 5

Set up an obstacle course around your house using everyday objects. Blindfold a family member, and lead him or her through the obstacle course using oral cues. Then talk about what it looks like for the Holy Spirit to guide us through each day.

CHALLENGE 6

Watch for at least three different instructions, and think of a way the Holy Spirit might guide you to serve someone through those instructions. For example, if you see a door with the word "pull" on it so you know which way it opens, you could then hold it open for someone else.

FOLLOW THE RECIPE

Take a look at the ingredients shown here. Create a simple recipe combining three different ingredients—and a few others if you'd like. Name your new creation! (Maybe later you can make your invention for your family.)

CHOCOLATE SYRUP

SUNFLOWER SEEDS

STRAWBERRIES

RAISINS

PRETZEL STICKS

MINI-MARSHMALLOWS

© ISTOCKPHOTO.COM: THOMAS PERKINS, TOTO8888, ANNA KUCHEROVA, DRACONUS, JAN GOTTWALD, TAMMY CROSSON

MY RECIPE

LAW OF THE LAND

List the name of your new land, the location of your new land, and a set of three rules that all your citizens must live by!

Land Name: _____

Location: _____

Rule #1: _____

Rule #2: _____

Rule #3: _____

WE WEAR THE ARMOR OF GOD

HONESTY IS...
telling the truth.

Ephesians 6:10-17:
The Armor of God

God gives us a full set of armor to help us fight the enemy, the devil. We can be strong in the Lord and stand firm in His power when we wear the belt of truth, the body armor of God's righteousness, the shoes of the good news of peace, the shield of faith, the helmet of salvation, and the sword of the Spirit. Use this lesson to help children learn to use God's armor to grow in honesty.

WHAT KIDS DO	WHAT YOU'LL NEED
God Sightings *(5 minutes)* Share ways they've seen God at work.	
Bible Experience *(10 minutes)* Learn about the armor of God and how it protects us.	• Bible • paper • belt, coat, slippers, winter cap • lid from a pot
God's Powerful Animals *(15 minutes)* Discover amazing strengths of God's animals, and consider how they need God's strength.	• Bible • 2 copies of the handout *(found at the end of this lesson)* • scissors
Depend on God *(10 minutes)* Imagine how aliens would operate objects, and consider how they depend on God.	• Bible
Protection Game *(10 minutes)* Have a paper fight.	• 5 sheets of paper per person
Life Application *(10 minutes)* Watch a video about the armor of God.	• *Character by God's Design* DVD • DVD player

ILLUSTRATION BY DREW ROSE

Photocopy the Take-Home page at the end of this lesson for each child.

HONESTY DEVOTION

In the Ephesians spiritual armor inventory, no piece exists that protects your back. God is calling you to stand and face your attacker head-on, face front. Thankfully, He doesn't kick you into the fray without protection. Choose one piece of armor to focus on. You might find that one "suits" your current situation perfectly. Visualize yourself putting on that piece of armor. Pray for understanding of how to wear it and use it effectively. Ask God to help you use that armor to stand firm against the enemy.

BIBLE FOUNDATION FOR TEACHERS

Ephesians 6:10-17: The Armor of God

DRESSING FOR BATTLE

In many video games, the first thing you must do is create an avatar or character. In fact, you can't play the game until you've chosen your human warrior, complete with armor for the ensuing battle, a variety of weapons, even a snazzy haircut. In Ephesians, we see that dressing for spiritual battle is as important as dressing for a physical battle. If you go into battle—virtual, spiritual, or otherwise—without all your armor, you'll never come out alive. The armor of God in Ephesians 6 covers us from head to toe for spiritual battle.

ARMED WITH TRUTH

The description of the armor of God implies that character, not brute force, wins the battle. The armor in Ephesians represents truth, righteousness, peace, faith, and salvation. The belt of truth is the first item listed, and the belt holds the weapons. Without truth and sincerity, there can be no victory. It's no coincidence the body armor (translated "breastplate" by some) of righteousness covers your heart. Decency, honesty, and virtue are synonyms for righteousness—and descriptions to which one's heart might aspire. Walk in peace as you put on the shoes of Good News. Completing your spiritual ensemble are helmet, shield, and sword—for cover, defense, and offense. Wear salvation as a helmet, enveloping your mind with thoughts of divine deliverance, rescue, and recovery. Your shield, crafted from pure faith, is able to block attacks meant to wound and burn. Stand firm as you wield God's Word as a sword, dividing truth from lies with one fell swoop.

ILLUSTRATION BY DANA REGAN

ENEMY INTEL

Once you've put on your armor, expect to use it. You can't get dressed for battle and expect to sit on the sidelines. In Ephesians, we see an attack that the devil uses: the fiery arrow. He uses these fiery arrows—insults, self-deprecating thoughts, doubts, lies—to wound us, to scar us. However, the shield of faith is the perfect article of armor to deflect and defend from such attacks. In Genesis 3:1-5, the devil twisted God's words, confusing Eve. The helmet of salvation combats these mind games. Satan used the same strategy in an effort to tempt Jesus in Matthew 4:1-11. Jesus counterattacked with the sharp edge of God's Word. At every turn, God has equipped us to defend, attack, and succeed. Together with shield, sword, and the full armor of God, we stand firm in victory.

GOD SIGHTINGS

As a group, share God Sightings—ways you've seen God at work. Then celebrate how God is at work in your lives through a prayer of thanksgiving.

BIBLE EXPERIENCE

Talk about: **In our battle to be honest and do the right thing, God has given us armor to protect us, head to toe! We're stronger when 👆 we wear the armor of God.** Ask for a volunteer.

Read Ephesians 6:10-12. Have kids fold paper airplanes and throw them at the volunteer and you like fiery arrows. Say: **We need some help! Let's see God's way of protecting us.**

Read Ephesians 6:13. As you read the following verses and explain each piece, put the clothing items on the child standing with you.

Read Ephesians 6:14. **The belt of truth** (belt) **holds your weapons and your armor together. The body armor, made from God's righteousness** (coat, put on backward), **protects your heart.**

Read Ephesians 6:15. **The shoes of Good News** (slippers) **give you peace, the gospel preparing you for your journey.**

THE LESSON

> ## YOU'LL NEED:
>
> ✓ **Bible**
> ✓ **paper**
> ✓ **belt**
> ✓ **coat**
> ✓ **slippers**
> ✓ **winter hat**
> ✓ **lid for a cooking pot**

Read Ephesians 6:16. **The shield** (lid for a cooking pot) **is your faith, your belief in what God says.**

Read Ephesians 6:17. **The helmet that comes from believing in Jesus** (winter cap) **protects your mind. The sword** (Bible) **is God's Word, which you use to fight Satan.**

Have kids toss their airplanes again, and encourage the "armored" child to block them using the Bible.

Lead this discussion: **Why do you like that God gave us this powerful armor? Choose one piece of armor (belt, body armor, shoes, helmet, shield, or sword), and tell how it can protect you. Talk about one piece of armor you need today—and why.**

Talk about: **God gives all of us exactly what we need to face our enemy and win the battle. To win, ● we wear the armor of God.**

GOD'S POWERFUL ANIMALS

See the Teacher Prep box in advance of this activity.

Talk about: **The armor of God keeps us safe. Name some things that help you feel safe and protected.**

Then ask: **What does it mean to wear the armor of God?**

Read Ephesians 6:10. **Let's see if we can figure out the strength of some of God's most powerful creatures.**

Shuffle and lay out the cards that you cut out from the handout. Instruct kids to work together to figure out which description fits with each animal. After several minutes, share the answers.

Lead this discussion: **How surprised were you about the power of some of God's creatures? What are some things you're strong enough to do by yourself? What are some things God's armor helps you do?**

Say: **We can be surprisingly strong with God's help when ● we wear the armor of God.**

✓ **Bible**

✓ **2 copies of the handout** *(found at the end of this lesson)*

✓ **scissors**

TEACHER PREP

In advance, copy the handout onto card stock. Then cut out each of the squares, shuffle them, and put them in a pile. Be sure to keep an uncut copy for your answer key.

DEPEND ON GOD

Say: **God gives us a full set of armor to help us fight against the enemy, the devil. Each piece of the armor of God is an important tool that we can use every day. We can be strong in the Lord and stand firm in His power when we wear the belt of truth, the body armor of God's righteousness, the shoes of the good news of peace, the shield of faith, the helmet of salvation, and the sword of the Spirit.**

Read Ephesians 6:10 again. Then ask: **What do you think it means to be "strong in the Lord"?**

Say: **Let's have some fun with objects that depend on us in order to operate.** In pairs, have kids find an object in the classroom (such as a stapler, a remote control, an iPod) and come up with a silly 60-second skit to show what it might look like if people from another planet came across that object and how they might use it incorrectly.

After the skits, lead this discussion: **What do we have to do to operate each of these objects? How are the objects dependent on us to work right? How are you dependent on God to be honest and do the right thing? How can the armor of God help you be honest? What can you do to remind yourself to wear the armor of God every day?**

Say: **We can't get anywhere when we don't know God or experience God's power. But when we know God, we wear the armor of God and are strong in His power!**

PROTECTION GAME

Ask everyone to find one classroom or personal item to represent a piece of the armor of God—for example, a backpack, a hat, or a clipboard.

Give every person five sheets of paper for making paper balls.

Explain the game: If someone gets hit by a paper ball, that person is out and must

sit down. However, if a person blocks a paper ball with a piece of armor, the person is safe.

Begin the paper fight, and play until only one person is left standing.

Then lead this discussion: **How would wearing a full set of armor in this game have helped? Why is it important to put on the whole armor of God every day?**

Say: **To stay safe from the enemy, the devil, we wear the armor of God.**

LIFE APPLICATION

Talk about: **In some video games, you can create a character or get better armor or even a stronger weapon if you do one thing: level up. Check out how these kids "level up" with the armor of God.**

Play "Level Up" (track 5) on the *Character by God's Design* DVD.

Afterward, lead this discussion: **What piece of armor in the video was your favorite? What did you like about it? Tell about a time you've used "armor" the way it was used in the video. In what ways can you use the full armor of God this week to be honest?**

Talk about: **We wear the armor of God for protection, to help guard our hearts and minds from the attacks of the enemy. God gives us exactly what we need to "level up" and win!**

PRAYER
Dear God, thank You for Your gift of armor to protect us. Please be with us and remind us to use Your armor and be honest. In Jesus' name, amen.

TAKE-HOME PAGE

Give each child a Take-Home page to take home. Encourage kids to select one of the six challenges for the week ahead.

YOU'LL NEED:

✓ *Character by God's Design* **DVD**
✓ **DVD player**

FOR TEACHERS:
TRUTH FROM PROVERBS

In the book of Proverbs, Solomon says those who are honest—those who do what's right in all situations, even when nobody's watching—discover that their honesty guides them in life. They know and do the truth.

PRACTICING HONESTY

Keep growing in your faith and character. Choose one of the following challenges to do this week to wear the armor of God.

CHALLENGE 1

With some friends, find some things to use as armor. Then play a game of Dodge Ball together. You can use your armor to deflect the ball. Afterward, talk about some different ways the devil may try to harm or trick us and how the armor of God protects us.

CHALLENGE 2

Draw a bunch of fiery arrows, and cut them out. Write on the backs of the arrows some different problems, evils, or temptations you face, and put the arrows on your wall. Pray that God will help you wear His armor and stand strong against fiery arrows from the devil.

CHALLENGE 3

Label items: "Helmet of Salvation" on a hat, "Body Armor of Righteousness" on a shirt, "Belt of Truth" on a belt, "Shield of Faith" on a book, "Shoes of Peace" on shoes, and "Sword of the Spirit" on a cardboard tube. Wear your "armor of God" and tell someone how each piece protects you.

CHALLENGE 4

Find a friend, and together use cardboard and aluminum foil to make your favorite pieces of armor. You might cover a belt or shoes in the foil or make a shield with the cardboard. Pretend to use your armor in a battle with your friend, and then talk about God's power.

CHALLENGE 5

When you put on your clothes, pretend you're putting on each piece of the armor of God. Then talk to God and ask Him to help you use the armor of God to stand firm against the devil.

CHALLENGE 6

With your friends or family, play a game of football, paintball, or any other sport that requires protective gear. After the game, talk about why the protective gear was important and why it's important to wear the full armor of God every day.

GOD'S POWERFUL ANIMALS

Eagle	Can lift something 4 times its own weight during flight.
Grizzly Bear	Can lift over 1,000 pounds!
Ox	Pulls things 1.5 times its weight across rugged terrain.
Tiger	Carries animals twice its own weight 10 feet up a tree.
Gorilla	Able to lift something that equals the weight of 30 adult humans!
African Elephant	The strongest mammal. Could carry the weight of 130 humans!
Leafcutter Ant	Can carry something 50 times its own body weight in its jaw!
Dung Beetle	Can pull 1,141 times its body weight; that's like person pulling 6 double-decker buses full of people.

Source: onekind.org

WE OBEY GOD'S WORD

OBEDIENCE IS...
doing what I'm told to do.

Psalm 119:
David Loves God's Word

The writer of Psalm 119 said he'd hidden God's Word inside his heart so it would always be a part of him. We can follow God's Word every day in all the things we do and say. Just as the writer of Psalm 119 did, we can learn to love the Bible as we discover the truths inside. God's Word is the light we need to guide our steps each day. Use this lesson to help children learn to obey God's Word.

WHAT KIDS DO	WHAT YOU'LL NEED
God Sightings *(5 minutes)* Share ways they've seen God at work.	
Bible Experience *(10 minutes)* Learn how hard it can be when we don't have the light of God.	• Bible • flashlight
Bible Verse Mobile *(15 minutes)* Create a mobile out of God's Word.	• Bibles • markers or crayons • index cards • hanger • string • scissors
Map to Guide Us *(5 minutes)* Learn how the Bible is like a map and how it can help us obey God.	• paper • colored pencils
Hidden Treasures *(15 minutes)* Write their favorite Scripture verses and hide them around the church.	• Bibles • large sticky notes • colored pencils
Life Application *(10 minutes)* Watch a video of someone who had to rely on God.	• *Character by God's Design* DVD • DVD player

ILLUSTRATION BY RONNIE ROONEY

*Photocopy the Take-Home page at the end of this lesson for each child.

OBEDIENCE DEVOTION

God wants us to keep His Word close to our hearts. Hiding God's Word in our hearts is an act of inner devotion. It results in delight at our very core but a delight that we share with others as we live our faith inside out. Pray that God will help you reveal His Word to the kids in your class this week. Ask Him to give your kids such a love for Him that they'll hide His Word in their hearts and follow it every day.

BIBLE FOUNDATION FOR TEACHERS

Psalm 119: David Loves God's Word

THE PSALM

Imagine pilgrims traveling on the dusty, sun-baked road to Jerusalem—or singers gathered on the Temple stone steps, eyes closed and voices raised. The songs and verses in Psalm 119 could've been sung by these people. They often expressed their devotion to God through music.

THE COMPOSITION

This particular psalm, the longest in the entire book, is as intricate as it is spiritual—following the Hebrew alphabet to the letter. Composed to be accompanied by a stringed instrument, a psalm is essentially a sacred song—and Psalm 119 was written especially artistically. Its construction of 22 sections, or "strophes," is unique, for each of the 22 strophes corresponds with a letter in the Hebrew alphabet. Each strophe is composed of eight lines or verses. If we read verses 9-16 in this psalm in Hebrew, we'd discover the first word in each line of the strophe begins with the Hebrew *beth* or "b." The psalmist was deliberate, poetic, and interested in the structure of this intricate song.

ILLUSTRATION BY DANA REGAN

THE WORDS

"I have hidden your word in my heart, that I might not sin against you." This psalmist, believed by many to be David, wrote throughout this strophe how important God's Word, commandments, and decrees were to him. He recited God's promises from the text out loud, studied His commandments, rejoiced in His laws, and delighted in God's decrees. The psalmist valued God's Word so much that it became as vital to his life as his own heart. This psalmist knew that the more he knew of God's ways, the less he'd rely on his own.

THE PURPOSE

"Hiding" God's Word is traditionally interpreted as memorizing it. While it may include repetition and recollection, it suggests an even deeper action of revering His Word in an intimate, personal way. "Hiding" suggests taking the life from God's Word and holding it in the deepest, innermost part of one's being. This portion of the psalm is complicated in construction but simple in purpose: God's Word, in our hearts, can keep us from straying from God.

THE LESSON

GOD SIGHTINGS

As a group, share God Sightings—ways you've seen God at work. Then celebrate how God is at work in your lives through a prayer of thanksgiving.

BIBLE EXPERIENCE

Read your favorite parts of Psalm 119.

Talk about: **We do all kinds of things every day. Brush our teeth, get dressed, maybe even smile! One thing to remember is ● we obey God's Word every day. God helps us understand how He wants us to live and tells us about His love for us. Let's explore the Bible a little deeper to find out how we can do just that.**

Have kids spread out around the room. Talk about: **Some of you are really good at remembering lines from your favorite movies. David—the boy shepherd who fought Goliath—could remember lines, too. He loved to hear what God had to say, and he remembered every word. Whenever he needed help or advice, he remembered God's words and knew just what to do. He even said that God's words were like a lamp to light the way.**

Tell kids they're going to try an experiment. You'll turn off the lights, and without talking, they'll try to find someone who's holding up the same number of fingers as them on one hand.

YOU'LL NEED:

✓ **Bible**
✓ **flashlight**

TEACHER TIP

This activity works best in a room that can be completely darkened.

Turn off the lights, and have kids silently try to find others. Then turn the flashlight on and off at irregular intervals, moving around the room and shining the light on kids to give them a quick glimpse of other kids' fingers. After two minutes, turn the lights back on.

Lead this discussion: **Talk about the difference between finding something in the dark and finding it in the light. How is God's Word like the flashlight? What would your life be like if you didn't have God's Word?**

Talk about: **When you're in the dark, it's hard to see what you're looking for. But the more we follow God's Word** (turn your flashlight on)**, the more we can live the way God wants us to. We want to see what God has for us every day, so ⬤ we obey God's Word every day.**

BIBLE VERSE MOBILE

Say: **The writer of Psalm 119 said he'd hidden God's Word inside his heart so it would always be a part of him. We can follow God's Word every day in all the things we do and say. Just as the writer of Psalm 119 did, we can learn to love the Bible as we discover the truths inside. God's Word is the light we need to guide our steps each day.**

Talk about: **There are things in God's Word that help us make good choices. Tell about a time or a situation where you made a good choice.**

Have kids each choose one of the following verses: Psalm 119:11, 12, 18, 57, 89, or 105, and write each word of the verse on a separate card.

Show them how to make a mobile with the cards by connecting each card to the hanger with different lengths of string.

Then lead this discussion: **Why is it important to remember God's Word? What are ways you can remember God's Word every day? What does it mean to you to hide God's Word in your heart? What are some ways we can follow God's Word every day?**

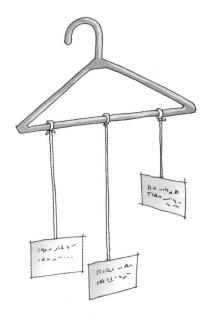

Say: **God's Word helps us know what He wants for our lives. The more we know the Bible, the more** **we obey God's Word every day.**

MAP TO GUIDE US

Say: **If you only told somebody the city you lived in, it'd be hard to find your house. Draw a map of your city. It doesn't have to be perfect, but see how well you can do.**

Distribute paper and colored pencils. Assist with map-making as needed.

As kids are working, ask: **How is finding a house by using a street map like finding a verse in the Bible?**

What are some ways you follow the Bible every day?

Say: **When we understand how the Bible is put together, it's easier to read and use. We can easily find and read verses and passages. When we can find what's in God's Word,** **we obey God's Word every day.**

HIDDEN TREASURES

Have each person pick a verse from the Bible and write it on large sticky note. As a group, walk around the classroom area of your church and hang the verses in various places so others will discover them.

Thank God for his Word and for helping you share it with others.

LIFE APPLICATION

Talk about: **We know the Bible helps us because God says it does. But we can also hear people talk about relying on the Bible. Let's watch a story of someone who had to rely on God's Word through a tough time.**

Watch "Everyday Word" (track 6) on the *Character by God's Design* DVD.

YOU'LL NEED:

✓ paper
✓ colored pencils

YOU'LL NEED:

✓ **Bibles**
✓ **large sticky notes**
✓ **colored pencils**

YOU'LL NEED:

✓ *Character by God's Design* **DVD**
✓ **DVD player**

Lead this discussion: **Talk about something amazing you learned from this video. What's something you've learned from God's Word? What's something from God's Word you can use every day?**

Talk about: ● **We obey God's Word every day. No matter what we're doing or where we're going, God's Word helps us make good decisions. Just as the man in this video learned a lesson about forgiveness, we learn things from God's Word that we can follow every day.**

PRAYER
Thank You, God, for the Bible, and for helping us follow what we learn from the Bible every day. In Jesus' name, amen.

TAKE-HOME PAGE

Give each child a Take-Home page to take home. Encourage kids to select one of the six challenges for the week ahead.

PRACTICING OBEDIENCE

Keep growing in your faith and character. Choose one of the following challenges to do this week to obey God's Word.

CHALLENGE 1
Find a Bible verse that can help you every day, and share it with a friend.

CHALLENGE 2
Write out Psalm 119:11 on three different cards, and hide each card in a family member's or friend's things (like your dad's briefcase or your mom's purse). As you hide the cards, think about hiding God's Word in your heart.

CHALLENGE 3
Carry a Bible with you throughout the week as a reminder to always be thinking about how God's Word helps you every day. When you have some free time, take a few minutes to read your Bible.

CHALLENGE 4
Interview your mom or dad, and ask about his or her favorite Bible verse. Find out why the verse is meaningful to your parent, and write it down. Later, read the verse on your own and think about what God wants you to learn from it.

CHALLENGE 5
Copy an entire psalm onto a piece of paper, and carry it with you this week. Whenever you have a spare moment, reread it.

CHALLENGE 6
Set aside time to read a chapter of 1 John. First John will help you learn how important it is to love others and how to put your faith in Jesus into action. After you read a chapter, write down one important truth you learned.

WE OBEY GOD NO MATTER WHAT

OBEDIENCE IS...
doing what I'm told to do.

God had very specific—and bizarre—instructions for Ezekiel. God used Ezekiel to illustrate what would happen to Jerusalem as its people were punished severely by God for their unfaithfulness. What's amazing is that Ezekiel was so willing to take on the pain of delivering this uncomfortable prophecy. Ezekiel obeyed God—no matter what. Use this lesson to help children to grow in their obedience to God—no matter what!

Ezekiel 2:2-3; 4:1–5:10:
Ezekiel Follows God's
Bizarre and Gross Orders

WHAT KIDS DO	WHAT YOU'LL NEED
God Sightings *(5 minutes)* Share ways they've seen God at work.	
Bible Experience *(10 minutes)* Use clay and the account of Ezekiel to think about obedience.	• Bible • modeling dough or clay • pencils
Motion Devotion *(10 minutes)* Make up motions to a song about obeying God.	
Zeke Trading Cards *(15 minutes)* Make Trading Cards as they examine Ezekiel's obedience.	• index cards • thin markers or colored pencils
Critter Crawl *(10 minutes)* Imitate animals and talk about what God wants them to do that makes them feel silly.	
Life Application *(10 minutes)* Do some bizarre actions, and consider Ezekiel's obedience.	• 3 sheets of paper • 3 coins • pencils or markers

ILLUSTRATION BY DREW ROSE

*Photocopy the Take-Home page at the end of this lesson for each child.

OBEDIENCE DEVOTION

Someone crossing a marathon finish line. A veteran public servant. Long-term dedication—you'll see it if you're looking.

When you see long-term dedication today, ask God how He's expecting you to express obedience throughout your lifetime. What does He want you to do—no matter what?

Ask God to inspire the kids in your class to catch hold of what it means to serve Him no matter what.

BIBLE FOUNDATION FOR TEACHERS

Ezekiel 2:2-3; 4:1–5:10: Ezekiel Follows God's Bizarre and Gross Orders

WHAT THE BIBLE SAYS

Chosen by God to be a prophet to Israel, Ezekiel received instructions from God to draw a map of Jerusalem on a clay brick and then construct models of siege ramps and battering rams around it.

God told Ezekiel to place an iron griddle between himself and the brick, turning toward the model and lying on his left side for 390 days—one day for each year of Israel's sin. God's next instruction was for Ezekiel to turn over and lie on his right side for 40 days.

During this time, Ezekiel would survive on tight rations: a measure of water and eight ounces of food daily, cooked over dried human dung. Yes, that's right—human feces. The fuel source prompted Ezekiel to ask God to substitute cow dung—handling human dung would make him defiled (and it was just gross!). God agreed to this compromise.

Further, Ezekiel had to shave his head and beard, and then divide his shaved hair into three equal parts. One third was to be placed on the center of the map, one third scattered across the map, and one third scattered to the wind or burned.

God used Ezekiel to illustrate what would happen to Jerusalem as its people were punished severely by God for their unfaithfulness. So extreme would be the punishment that families would resort to cannibalism.

WHAT IT MEANS

Wow...other prophets got to walk into throne rooms and make announcements. But Ezekiel? He had to shave his head and beard and lie on the ground unmoving for more than 14 months, practically starving. And what a message to share: Harsh times were coming.

The symbolism of Ezekiel's actions was clear: A deadly siege of Jerusalem was in the future—a siege in which there would be severe shortages of food and water. People would die from war, famine, and disease.

What's amazing is that Ezekiel was so willing to take on the pain of delivering this uncomfortable prophecy. Ezekiel obeyed God—no matter what.

WHY IT MATTERS

It would've been easy for Ezekiel to stride into a palace, strike a heroic pose, and deliver a ringing denouncement of Israel. But God wanted His prophecy to be acted out—and even with each day symbolizing a whole year of disobedience, those days added up.

In some situations obeying God is quick, if not always easy—walking away from a temptation or refusing to participate in something illegal, for instance. But other times obedience calls for long-term dedication, such as keeping yourself pure sexually, treating your body with the same care with which God created it, or being honest in a dishonest world.

Ezekiel decided to serve God no matter what, however long God asked him to serve.

GOD SIGHTINGS

THE LESSON

As a group, share God Sightings—ways you've seen God at work. Then celebrate how God is at work in your lives through a prayer of thanksgiving.

✓ **Bible**
✓ **modeling dough or clay**
✓ **pencils**

BIBLE EXPERIENCE

Read Ezekiel 2:2-3; 4:1–5:10.

Talk about: **Ezekiel was a prophet who lived during a time when God's people had ignored Him and were in trouble. God gave special messages to the people through Ezekiel... with some strange and pretty gross instructions.**

Hand out modeling clay and pencils. Talk about: **First God told Ezekiel to draw on a clay brick the city of Jerusalem under attack. Sculpt a brick, and draw on it something that's important to you. Imagine how sad Ezekiel was to learn that his home city of Jerusalem would be captured.** Have kids show their bricks.

Talk about: **Next, God told Ezekiel to lie down on one side for more than a year! God said that this symbolized Ezekiel bearing the sins of the people of Israel. Use your clay to sculpt a few friends.** Pause. **Imagine what it'd like if you had to pay for all the sins your friends ever committed.**

Talk about: **To show hard times ahead, God told Ezekiel to eat bread cooked over poop. Gross! And Ezekiel could only drink a small amount of water. Sculpt something you'd really miss if you couldn't eat or drink it any more.** Have kids show their sculptures.

Talk about: **God also told Ezekiel to divide up his hair, burn some of it, and scatter the rest. The hair represented the Israelites. Some of them would die, and the rest would have to live far away from their families and friends, because they'd ignored God. Break your clay into small pieces.** Pause.

Talk about: **All these weird instructions were to show the Israelites that they'd ignored God and would be punished. Sculpt as you silently talk to God, asking for forgiveness for ways you've ignored Him. As you pray, remember that ● we obey God no matter what.** Allow time for prayer.

MOTION DEVOTION

Say: **God had very specific—and bizarre—instructions for Ezekiel to warn the people in Jerusalem. Ezekiel obeyed God no matter what.**

In pairs, have kids talk about each of these questions. Ask for volunteers to share responses with the group before moving on to the next question.

- **What do you think about what God told Ezekiel to do?**

- **What was the hardest thing God told Ezekiel to do?**

- **What's the hardest thing God has told you to do?**

- **What helps you do hard things to obey God no matter what?**

Then say: **The Bible is full of songs that people sang about obeying God—and how sometimes it could be hard to obey. With your partner, come up with motions to this song:**

"If You Love Me and You Know It" to the tune of "If You're Happy and You Know It."

**If you love me and you know it, just obey.
If you love me and you know it, just obey.
If you love me and you know it, to obey will really show it.
If you love me and you know it, just obey.**

Encourage kids to come up with unusual or unexpected motions. Then sing the song together with motions!

Lead this discussion: **What makes it hard for kids your age to obey God? How does obeying God show you love Him?**

Say: **God wants us to obey Him. Sometimes it may seem hard to obey God. It sure must've seemed that way to Ezekiel! But Ezekiel obeyed God, no matter what. We obey God no matter what, too. Think of this song when you run into a situation where it might be hard to obey God.**

✓ index cards

✓ thin markers or colored pencils

ZEKE'S TRADING CARDS

Talk about: **God had very specific—and bizarre—instructions for Ezekiel. What was the grossest command God gave Ezekiel?**

Say: **God gave Ezekiel some strange commands, such as drawing a map on a brick and cutting his hair. Here's a gross command God gave him: to eat bread that had been cooked over poop. But the command that was probably the most uncomfortable was to lie on his side for over a year. Let's imagine what that would be like.**

Have kids lie completely still on their left side for several minutes. As they lie there, ask them to call out some sins people commit. Make sure they don't forget disobeying, murdering, stealing, lying, saying bad words, being mean, being rude, ignoring God, being selfish, being greedy, ignoring someone who needs help, cheating, and being disrespectful.

After several minutes, have kids sit up.

Lead this discussion: **What did it feel like to lie on your side and hear all those sins called out? Tell about a time you felt uncomfortable. Explain whether you'd be willing to be that uncomfortable for over a year to show people they were sinning.**

Hand out index cards and markers and say: **Trading cards have famous people—usually sports stars—on them. Well, Ezekiel was a star, too. On your index card, design a trading card featuring Ezekiel as the star. Try to show in your picture how he obeyed God.**

Let kids share their finished work. Then lead this discussion: **What kinds of people often get star treatment? In our society, why do you think we don't treat people who obey God's commands like stars? Explain whether it's easier or harder to obey God knowing it might make you unpopular.**

Say: **Obeying God is so important that there ought to be star cards for people who obey. Often it seems as though it's the people who *don't* obey God who get the star** treatment. But don't worry. God knows when  we obey God no matter what. And that's what counts!

CRITTER CRAWL

Tell children you're going to have them act and sound like animals. Call out the following animals: monkey, shrimp, toucan, lion, zebra, ant, manatee, hummingbird, sucker-footed bat... or add your own! Keep the game moving by changing animals every 10 to 15 seconds.

Then lead this discussion: **Talk about how silly you felt playing this game. Share about a time you didn't do something because you were afraid of how you'd look. Tell about something God wants you to do that makes you feel kind of silly.**

Say: **Even when it means being different from others, we obey God no matter what.**

LIFE APPLICATION

Talk about: **God's orders probably seemed really weird to Ezekiel. But he obeyed them, no matter what. Thankfully, most of the commands God wants us to obey—like loving, forgiving, being nice, telling the truth—aren't weird or gross at all.**

Work together with kids to create three papers—each with a grid of nine squares. (See sample.) In each square, write...

Paper 1: Body actions, such as standing on one foot

Paper 2: Sound effects, such as clucking like a chicken

Paper 3: Simple tasks, such as crumpling a sheet of paper

When finished, form a circle and place the three grids in the middle. Have someone toss a coin onto each paper to select a square. Then combine the three actions into a command for everyone to do. For example, your command might be "While standing on one foot, cluck like a chicken, and crumple a piece of paper."

YOU'LL NEED:

✓ **3 sheets of paper**

✓ **3 coins**

✓ **pencils or markers**

Dance	Stand on one leg	Wave your arms
Wiggle your fingers	Shake your legs	Tap your toes
March in place	Nod your head	Shrug your shoulders

After several rounds, lead this discussion: **Which commands in this game were the most bizarre to act out? Which of God's commands to Ezekiel were the most bizarre to you? What instructions from God seem sort of bizarre to you today? How do you think most people look at commands from God such as "put others first" or "love your enemies"?**

Talk about: **Ezekiel obeyed God's strange and gross commands to make a point for God. And we know that there's always a good reason for God's commands. Even when God's commands seem strange, ● we obey God no matter what.**

PRAYER

God, thank You for giving us Ezekiel's example of a man who obeyed You no matter what. Please help us in everything we do to obey You no matter what. In Jesus' name, amen.

TAKE-HOME PAGE

Give each child a Take-Home page to take home. Encourage kids to select one of the six challenges for the week ahead.

PRACTICING OBEDIENCE

Keep growing in your faith and character. Choose one of the following challenges to do this week to show God you'll obey Him no matter what.

CHALLENGE 1
Teach someone in your family or a friend the words and motions to "If You Love Me and You Know It."

CHALLENGE 2
Find the grossest place in your house and tell God there that you'll obey Him no matter what!

CHALLENGE 3
Whenever someone says that something is gross, say, "If you think that's gross, listen to this…" and tell them about what you learned about Ezekiel.

CHALLENGE 4
Show your Ezekiel trading card to a friend and family member and tell why Ezekiel was a star in God's eyes.

CHALLENGE 5
Imagine the most unusual place that you could live to serve God. Write a story or draw a picture of that place.

CHALLENGE 6
Ask God to show you any area in your life where you haven't been obeying Him. Confess your sin to God and obey no matter what.

WE PLEASE GOD WHEN WE OBEY

OBEDIENCE IS...
doing what I'm told to do.

Matthew 3:1-6;
Galatians 3:26-27:
John Baptizes People
in the Jordan River

John the Baptist was able to show people how to please God by encouraging them to ask for forgiveness, turn from their sin, and be baptized. John the Baptist baptized people in the river after they repented of their sins. Those people decided to turn away from bad things and obey God. Use this lesson to help children learn that they can please God by obeying Him, too.

WHAT KIDS DO	WHAT YOU'LL NEED
God Sightings (*5 minutes*) Share ways they've seen God at work.	
Bible Experience (*10 minutes*) Read a Bible passage and experience different aspects of obedience.	• Bible • bookmark • spoons • small cups of honey • scratchy fabric • spray bottle with water
Obedient Eggs (*10 minutes*) Learn how things in their life can keep them from obeying God.	• plastic eggs, taped shut (*put water in half of them*) • cups
Faith in Action (*15 minutes*) Discover connections between rules and obedience.	• Bibles • copies of the handout (*found at the end of this lesson*) • pencils • markers or crayons
Obey and Play (*10 minutes*) Make up their own rules to a game.	• any familiar game
Life Application (*10 minutes*) Learn a creative way to introduce the idea of obedience.	• paper • markers

ILLUSTRATION BY PAMELA JOHNSON

Photocopy the Take-Home page at the end of this lesson for each child.

103

OBEDIENCE DEVOTION

We live in a culture that celebrates success and rewards ambition. John's message of humility is just as important for us as it was for the original hearers. What in your life are you holding on to as a testament to your own merit? How can you give God the glory for your accomplishments? Pray that, like John, your focus can be on preparing your heart for God rather than any worldly ambition and that you can live a humble lifestyle that will lead others to the kingdom of heaven.

BIBLE FOUNDATION FOR TEACHERS

Matthew 3:1-6; Galatians 3:26-27: John Baptizes People in the Jordan River

A VOICE IN THE WILDERNESS

John the Baptist lived a very simple, restricted life in the desert while he preached about the coming of Jesus. Without hesitation, John gave out strong warnings to the people to repent of their sinful ways. He spoke of someone who was coming soon—Jesus— who would be greater than John himself. He encouraged anyone who would listen to prepare the way for the Lord. John likely lived in the desert so he could preach and baptize without restrictions from local leaders. It was a natural place for true prophets, a place where the holy could draw large crowds and exclude themselves from the confines of corrupt governments. For John, the wilderness also had another meaning—he was preparing the Jews for a new exodus, in which they would find freedom even greater than being released from the hand of Pharaoh. Through Jesus, they would find the freedom from sin.

ILLUSTRATION BY PAIGE BILLIN-FRYE

LOCUSTS AND HONEY

John's lifestyle matched his preaching. He gave up traditional food for a diet of locusts and honey, dressed in rough and unfashionable clothes, and deprived himself of comfort, possessions, and status. Like a first-century Mother Teresa, he aligned himself with the poor. His coarse clothing was typical of the poor in his day. Likewise, his diet was typical of the poor. Honey was a readily available sweetener, even to the poor, and locusts weren't unusual in the diet of the lower class. Through his example, John called people not only to repent of their sins but also to reprioritize their lives and live a new life in Christ.

BAPTISM IN THE JORDAN

In the midst of learning about how the church is a united body, we look at one of the most controversial topics among Christians: baptism. However, the core of the issue isn't about infant versus adult baptism, or sprinkling versus immersion. It's not about the nuances of the traditions and meaning of baptism. The important thing is that, even before Jesus began His ministry, baptism was a symbol of a new life. It was the way John's followers showed that they were prepared for the Lord's coming.

HUMBLE YOURSELVES

John's lifestyle showed people that following Jesus required sacrifice and a change in the way they lived. John's lifestyle was humble—much more humble than one would expect for the son of a priest. His humble lifestyle was a symbol of how unworthy he was compared to the amazing Messiah. With his radical message, John set an example for all those who would follow him: Live humbly, make sacrifices, and simply follow Jesus.

THE LESSON

GOD SIGHTINGS

As a group, share God Sightings—ways you've seen God at work. Then celebrate how God is at work in your lives through a prayer of thanksgiving.

BIBLE EXPERIENCE

See the Teacher Prep box on the next page in advance of the activity.

Talk about: **God called John the Baptist to tell people to turn away from sin and be baptized. Because John obeyed God, many other people did, too.** ● **We please God when we obey.**

Say: **I'll have one of you read the Bible passage but when I hold up my hand, our reader will stop so we can experience that part of the passage.** Have a child read Matthew 3:1-6 and Galatians 3:26-27 slowly.

After Matthew 3:3, have kids cup their hands around their mouths and shout, "The Lord's coming!"

YOU'LL NEED:

✓ **Bible**
✓ **bookmark**
✓ **spoons**
✓ **small cups of honey**
✓ **scratchy fabric**
✓ **spray bottle with water**

Put bookmarks in your Bible so it's easy for the child to find Matthew 3:1-6 and Galatians 3:26-27.

Put a small amount of honey in each cup.

After the description of clothes in verse 4, pass scratchy fabric around and have kids feel the rough texture.

After the description of food, have kids taste the honey in the cup.

After verse 6, use a spray bottle to lightly mist the kids with water.

After Galatians 3:27, have kids act out putting on pants and shirts.

Talk about: **John the Baptist was called to prepare the way for Jesus—and he obeyed by preaching in the wilderness. It wasn't an easy life. But he was excited about following God! And he paid careful attention to God and His Word so he knew what to do.**

Lead this discussion: **Explain which of John's actions seem the weirdest to you. What things did we do that made you uncomfortable? How might obeying God make you feel weird or uncomfortable? What makes obedience worth it?**

Talk about: **God likes it when we obey, the way John did in the Bible passage. As we listened to the passage, we had to pay careful attention so we'd know what to do, and life can be like that, too. Let's always be aware and pay attention because ● we please God when we obey.**

OBEDIENT EGGS

Put water in half of the plastic eggs. Tape the eggs shut so kids can't open them until told.

The eggs spin best on a hard, flat surface.

See the Teacher Prep box in advance of this activity.

Say: **John the Baptist was able to show people how to please God by encouraging them to ask for forgiveness, turn from their sin, and be baptized. We please God when we obey, just as the people who were baptized pleased God by obeying.**

Have kids turn to a partner and share about a time they think they pleased God. Then invite volunteers to share their responses.

Hand out the plastic eggs you prepared in advance. Tell kids: **Don't open these eggs until you're told!**

Say: **Some of these eggs are going to obey you today, and some of them aren't. Spin your egg on its wide end.**

Assist as needed. Let kids try each other's eggs.

Ask: **Why do you think some eggs would spin and others wouldn't?**

Have kids open their eggs over a cup.

Lead this discussion: **What kept some of the eggs from spinning? What kinds of things keep you from obeying God? How can you avoid letting those things keep you from obeying God today?**

Say: **The water hidden in some of the eggs kept them from spinning. Sometimes there are things in our lives that keep us from obeying. Ask God to help you take those things out of your life, like you took the water out of our eggs.**

Today, you'll be faced with times you'll have to decide whether to obey God or not. Remember that  **we please God when we obey.**

FAITH IN ACTION

Say: **John the Baptist baptized people in the river after they repented of their sins. Those people decided to turn away from bad things and obey God.**

In the top box on their handouts, have kids draw a picture of a baptism they saw or experienced.

When kids are finished drawing, say: **Now find three items around you that have to do with rules. These might have to do with someone who gives you rules, a place you have rules, or a rule you have to follow. Write the things and rules on your handout.**

Lead this discussion: **What was it like to figure out the rules for the items? How is that like or unlike figuring out what God wants you to do? What helps you know the rules God and teachers and your parents have for you?**

Say: **Sometimes it might seem like we have to guess how to obey God. But God is clear in the Bible about how to obey, and He shows us in our hearts what's right. Let's**

YOU'LL NEED:

✓ **Bibles**
✓ **copies of the handout** *(found at the end of this lesson)*
✓ **pencils**
✓ **markers or crayons**

seek to really know God and hear Him because  we please God when we obey.

Read Hebrews 11, and have kids follow along in their Bibles. As you do, have them list the people and how they pleased God by their obedience on their handouts.

Talk about: **How can you apply what you learned from Hebrews 11 today?**

Say: **A great way to find out how to obey God is to read His Word, the Bible.** We please God when we obey.

OBEY AND PLAY

Choose a quick game your whole class knows how to play. Have each person make up his or her own rules for the game, but not tell anyone else what the made-up rules are.

Play the game with everyone's own rules.

Then lead this discussion: **Why didn't (or did) it work to have your own rules? How does having just one set of rules make it easier to play a game? What information has God given us in the Bible about how to live our lives? Why does He want us to obey the things He tells us to do?**

Say: **Maybe it doesn't seem fair or even fun at the time, but we have to trust God.** We please God when we obey.

LIFE APPLICATION

Kids' only mission during this activity is to pay attention and follow directions. Give kids the following directions in this order:

- **Get a piece of paper and grab a marker.**
- **Draw a V on the right side of the paper.**
- **Draw an O on the left side of the paper.**

- On the right side of the O, draw a line straight up and down.

- Left of the V, draw three left-to-right lines, one above the other.

- Draw a straight up-and-down line, connecting the left ends of the three lines you just drew.

- Draw a line straight down from the bottom point of the V.

- Draw a number three connected to the right side of the line next to the O.

Say: **If you obeyed my instructions, you'll have a word on your page. Let's all shout it together. One, two, three, "OBEY!"**

Lead this discussion: **Explain if you thought I had a plan for the drawing or if you thought I was giving random instructions. Why is it important to obey, even if you don't know the reasons? Tell about a time you didn't know why you had to do something, but you obeyed anyway.**

Talk about: **You didn't know why I was asking you to follow the directions I gave you, but in the end you came up with a neat result! Sometimes obeying your parents or obeying God is like that—you end up with something great because you obeyed. God has a plan for us, so ● we please God when we obey.**

PRAYER
Thank You, God, for new life through Jesus and for teaching us how to obey You. In Jesus' name, amen.

TAKE-HOME PAGE

Give each child a Take-Home page to take home. Encourage kids to select one of the six challenges for the week ahead.

PRACTICING OBEDIENCE

Keep growing in your faith and character. Choose one of the following challenges to do this week to show God you can obey Him.

CHALLENGE 1

Read Exodus 20:1-17 in the Bible. Think about what you can do to obey the commands you read. Do your best to obey those commands this week.

CHALLENGE 2

Ask an adult to take you to the library to check out *The Tale of Peter Rabbit* by Beatrix Potter. Read the book with the adult, and then discuss how things could have gone differently for Peter Rabbit had he obeyed and pleased his mother. Share one thing you could do differently to obey your parents.

CHALLENGE 3

Think of something your parents often have to tell you to do more than once before you obey. Write it down on a piece of paper and stick it in your pocket to remind you to do that thing even before it's asked of you.

CHALLENGE 4

Get some paper and draw water across the bottom with several big waves. Make the choice to obey God in some way, and write a word to describe what you did inside one wave. After several instances of obedience, you'll have a word in each wave. Finish the picture by drawing a scene with John the Baptist baptizing people in the water.

CHALLENGE 5

The people John baptized turned away from their sins and obeyed God. Grab a friend or family member and a spinning top. Spin the top and name a sin that someone your age might be tempted to do. Then let the other person spin the top the other way and name a way to turn away from that sin. Play until you can't think of any more sins.

CHALLENGE 6

It pleases God when we obey Him. Keep a "smiley-face journal" by writing down specific ways you obeyed God this week. Then write why your obedience in that way might have pleased God. Beside each entry, draw a smile or add a smiley sticker.

FAITH IN ACTION

RULES:

1. _____

2. _____

3. _____

BIBLE PEOPLE	OBEDIENCE

WE LEARN HOW TO LIVE FROM THE BIBLE

OBEDIENCE IS...
doing what I'm told to do.

If we read the Bible, we grow stronger as Christians. God's Word can help us with all we need. When we need to learn about God, when we need help with decisions or problems, we can read the Bible. Use this lesson to help children discover that we learn how to live from the Bible.

Hebrews 5:11–6:3:
Paul Explains How
Christians Grow Strong

WHAT KIDS DO	WHAT YOU'LL NEED
God Sightings *(5 minutes)* Share ways they've seen God at work.	
Bible Experience *(10 minutes)* Learn how to obey when they're being distracted.	• Bible • paper • markers
Exercise Your Faith *(10 minutes)* Connect reading their Bibles to exercise.	• Bible • timer with an alarm
Mark My Words *(20 minutes)* In pairs, go in-depth and annotate Bible passages.	• Bibles *(or copies of Matthew 5 that kids can highlight)* • colored highlighters
Wisdom for You *(5 minutes)* Discuss how wisdom from the Bible helps their lives.	• Bibles
Life Application *(10 minutes)* Look at Scriptures and talk about how the Bible helps us.	• Bibles

ILLUSTRATION BY RONNIE ROONEY

Photocopy the Take-Home page at the end of this lesson for each child.

OBEDIENCE DEVOTION

Consider life's distractions and whether they've pulled you away from God's Word. Renew your relationship with Jesus by exploring Scriptures in a fresh, new way. Spend time in God's Word so you'll grow not only in your Christian walk but also in your role as a guide for kids. They'll see your desire to get to know Jesus better and follow suit.

BIBLE FOUNDATION FOR TEACHERS

Hebrews 5:11–6:3: Paul Explains How Christians Grow Strong

FROM/TO

The book of Hebrews is a letter, though the author never identifies himself. Some believe the writer was the Apostle Paul. Other scholars suggest Barnabas, a close friend of Paul and fellow traveler among the early churches, or Apollos, an intellectual who also associated with Paul. We do know the recipients of the letter were Jewish Christians who were struggling in their faith, possibly even considering a return to Judaism.

A LETTER OF WARNING

The purpose of the book of Hebrews was to warn Jewish converts against falling away from their faith and to remind them once again that the Old Testament points to Jesus as the promised Messiah sent by God to die for our sins. A portion in Hebrews 5–6 focuses on the danger of turning back to the old Jewish system with an accusation that Jewish Christians were being spiritually dull and slow to listen. By this time in their Christian walk, the recipients should've been teaching others, but their growth seemed stunted since they continued to need basic teachings themselves. This spiritual sluggishness was especially troubling because these were not recent converts. They knew better and they weren't progressing, evidenced by their childish approach to Christianity.

HOPE FOR THE CONVERTS

Even amid his rebuke, the author offered encouragement. He urged the converts to stop retreading the basics and to press on toward maturity in their understanding of God's Word instead. In

ILLUSTRATION BY DANA REGAN

today's vernacular, "You got it. You already know what to do. Stop second-guessing yourselves, and, God willing, let's move on."

HOPE FOR US

We're not very different from the early Jewish Christians in that we're all tempted by laziness. Just as with the early converts, the "I'll stick to what I know because it's easy and familiar" line of thinking can creep into us. God can help us move toward spiritual growth and maturity—but it takes effort on our part as well. For Christians today, the entire Scriptures are readily available. We know the Bible is our guidebook for new life in Christ, and we understand the Bible can make a real difference in our lives—if we study and apply it.

THE LESSON

GOD SIGHTINGS

As a group, share God Sightings—ways you've seen God at work. Then celebrate how God is at work in your lives through a prayer of thanksgiving.

BIBLE EXPERIENCE

Talk about: **It's frustrating to be told to do something when you don't understand how to do it. God doesn't do that. When God tells us to do something, He gives us clear instructions. God's Word is the Bible, and ● we learn how to live from the Bible.**

Say: **Has anyone ever said to you, "You're just not listening"? If so, you're not alone.** Read Hebrews 5:11-12.

Talk about: **This letter was written to some of the very first Christians. They stopped listening because they thought they knew everything about Jesus already. The person who wrote this letter told them they should be eating steak by now—and they were still only drinking milk like a baby!** Read Hebrews 5:13-14.

Choose one child to be the "Instructor." Distribute markers and paper to each person, and say: **Let's try something. You'll draw a detailed picture, but only what the Instructor tells you to draw. And I want you to talk or sing while the Instructor talks the entire time about what you should**

YOU'LL NEED:

✓ **Bible**

✓ **paper**

✓ **markers**

draw. Talk about yourself, sing your favorite song...
anything you want. Let the Instructor come up with any creative
step-by-step instructions for the drawing. Have kids hold up their
drawings at the end.

Afterward, lead this discussion: **What was it like to give or
follow directions with all the noise? What would've made it
easier for you to follow directions? What makes it difficult
to pay attention when God gives us directions?**

Read Hebrews 6:1-3. Talk about: ● **We learn how to live from
the Bible, God's Word. And God has so many wonderful
things to tell us! But sometimes we get distracted or stop
listening. The letter in Hebrews told the early Christians to
move on, to start listening and learn new things. We might
at times be like those early Christians and think there's
nothing else for us to learn. But God wants us to pay
close attention to what He says in the Bible because His
directions help us grow as Christians.**

EXERCISE YOUR FAITH

YOU'LL NEED:

✓ **Bible**
✓ **timer with an alarm**

Say: **If we read the Bible, we grow stronger as Christians.
God's Word can help us with all we need. When we need
to learn about God, when we need help with decisions or
problems, we can read the Bible.**

Talk about: **What are some ways you get your body strong?**

Set a timer for 30 seconds for each of the following activities.
Have kids do the action until they hear the alarm to stop.

• **toe-touch stretch**

• **jumping jacks**

• **eyebrow lift**

• **one-foot hop**

Lead this discussion: **How easy or hard were these exercises?
What "exercises" can you do with your Bible to make your
faith strong?**

Say: ● We learn how to live from the Bible. The Bible makes us strong spiritually. God wants us to read His Word so we become stronger on the inside.

Read Psalm 119:105. Lead kids in finishing their exercise with a 30-second stretch, like a plant reaching for the sun.

Lead this discussion: **A plant grows best with water and light. How is sunlight for the plant like the Bible for us? How can reading the Bible help us grow as Christians?**

Say: **The Bible helps us, teaches us, and strengthens us. When we spend time every day reading the Bible, we're allowing God's light to shine on us.**

MARK MY WORDS

Talk about: **God's Word can help us with all we need. What's something you've learned from the Bible that's helped you?**

Have kids pair up for this activity. Say: **Studying God's Word can be exciting and fun because it helps us learn how to live. Open your Bible to Matthew 5 (or refer to your paper copy) and follow these instructions.**

- **Highlight in yellow every mention of God as Father.**

- **Draw orange squiggles under any words or phrases that tell you what God is like.**

- **Put a green square around any words or phrases that tell you something that God does.**

- **Put a pink circle around any words or phrases that talk about how to live.**

- **Underline in blue the word or phrase you think is most important.**

Lead this discussion: **What did you like about studying the Bible this way? What things did you discover that'll help you today? Why is it important to follow what you've learned?**

Say: ● **We learn how to live from the Bible, God's Word.**

YOU'LL NEED:

✓ **Bibles (or copies of Matthew 5 that kids can highlight)**

✓ **colored highlighters**

WISDOM FOR YOU

Read Proverbs 2:1-11 together.

Lead this discussion: **In what ways does the Bible help us know how to live better? Share some things that you'd like to change.**

Pray together that God would help you do those things as you learn how to live from the Bible.

LIFE APPLICATION

Talk about: **The Bible is God's Word, and it was written to help us get to know God.** Pause to leaf quickly through a Bible. **There are 31,173 verses in the Bible—that's a lot! Let's look at six of these verses; they're good examples of how** ● **we learn how to live from the Bible.**

Assign the following verses to children to look up in the Bible: Luke 6:31; Philippians 4:6; 2 Corinthians 5:17; Matthew 11:28; Isaiah 41:10; and Psalm 37:8.

Have children each read their verse and tell what it means in their own words. Pair readers and nonreaders as necessary.

Afterward, lead this discussion: **Talk about which verse meant the most to you. How can that verse help you learn how to live? What are ways we can share God's Word with others?**

Talk about: **We explored some great verses from the Bible, and there are many more that help us grow. We want to know what God's Word says because** ● **we learn how to live from the Bible.**

PRAYER
God, thank You for Your Word—the Bible. We're grateful that You've given us everything we need to learn how to live. In Jesus' name, amen.

TAKE-HOME PAGE

Give each child a Take-Home page to take home. Encourage kids to select one of the six challenges for the week ahead.

PRACTICING OBEDIENCE

Keep growing in your faith and character. Choose one of the following challenges to do this week to learn how to live from the Bible.

CHALLENGE 1
With a family member, read Matthew 22:37-39. Talk about what you learned from these verses and how they'll help you in your everyday life.

CHALLENGE 2
Write out Philippians 4:13 on a notecard. Read it throughout the week and remember where your strength comes from.

CHALLENGE 3
Think of a friend who doesn't know Jesus. Write a favorite Bible verse on a card and give it to your friend for encouragement. (You might pick John 3:16 or Proverbs 3:5-6.)

CHALLENGE 4
Send a thank-you note to someone who's a spiritual leader in your life, and include a Bible verse you like. In the note, thank the person for helping you understand the Bible and helping you grow stronger as a Christian.

CHALLENGE 5
Ask a friend to be your "Bible Buddy." Together, read one chapter of the Bible, such as John 3; 1 Corinthians 13; Philippians 2; or Hebrews 11. Then talk about the chapter in person, on the phone, or by email. Share questions and discuss ways you can learn how to live from that chapter.

CHALLENGE 6
Keep a "Learning How to Live" journal. Each day when you read a verse or section in the Bible, ask yourself, *How does God want me to put this truth into action in my everyday life?* Then write one specific action you can take.